GO LIVE YOUR
ADVENTURE

CHOOSING EXPERIENCES THAT SHAPE YOU

KONAN STEPHENS

GO LIVE YOUR ADVENTURE

6305 Waterloo Road NW
Canal Winchester OH 43110

Copyright © 2021 by Konan Stephens

ISBN 978-0-578-93838-7
First Edition 2021

Design: Lydia Tarleton
Cover Photo: Rick Camacho

Printed in the United States of America 2021

ENDORSEMENTS

Live the story you would want to read. That's a statement I often remind myself of whenever I'm competing beyond my known abilities. A bike race such as the 2,700 mile-long Tour Divide inevitably etches a surreal story in the lives of its' competitors. Konan has not only lived his story, but his book reminds and inspires me to go out and live more grand stories of my own—to go live more of my own adventure!"

JOSH KATO
2015 Tour Divide Winner

"Start reading on page 11–that will tell you that Konan did not write a platitudinous book. This is a firsthand personal message of encouragement titled so very appropriately, *Go Live Your Adventure*. I have known Konan since the late 90s. He is a man of purpose, a leader with integrity and a heart to encourage others. Most importantly, he loves Jesus. You'll not read this book alone, you will share with your small group, friends, and family. Go, live your adventure!"

SAM CHAND
Author and Leadership Consultant
www.samchand.com

"Konan Stephens hit a huge home run with his latest book, Go Live Your Adventure. It is full of energy and inspiration. The stories, concepts, and illustrations will motivate you to live your best life. Do yourself a favor and grab a copy of his book. I'm certain that you'll be glad you did."

CHRIS SONKSEN
Founder of Church Boom
Pastor of South Hills
Author

Whatever he's got, I want it. That's the first thing I remember thinking when I met Konan Stephens for the first time. From that moment, I've had the privilege of watching him dominate so many crazy adventures that most people would never even attempt. Just watching his approach to life has been one of the greatest joys of my own life. This book outlines his life of adventure but also gives you the keys to unlock your own personal one. And oh, by the way, I did end up getting what he had—and my life is so much more exciting because of it!

GARY FOWLER
Best Friend
Life Coach and Leadership Consultant

TABLE OF CONTENTS

ADVENTURE #1: 100-MILE ULTRA

ADVENTURE #2: THE TOUR DIVIDE

ADVENTURE #3: THE GRAND CANYON RIM TO RIM TO RIM

ADVENTURE #4: CLIMBING KILIMANJARO

ADVENTURE #5: THE GREATEST ADVENTURE

FOREWORD

BY E. KEITH STEPHENS
[DAD]

I am so honored to have the privilege of writing the foreword for this book. I am Konan's Dad and, of course, have walked through most of life with him. When Konan was growing up, I warned him about the challenges we all face in life. He believed me and fortunately was able to skip through a lot of hardships before they ever happened. That's just who Konan is: very teachable, very driven, and always giving 100% to everything he does.

It was easy to tell that Konan was a competitor at a young age. During youth sports, he always played harder than all the other kids because he wanted to win so badly. He's always had a competitive edge. That edge took him from holding the first place trophy over his head at his first big wheel race in kindergarten to holding his mountain bike over his head after riding 2,700 miles from Canada to Mexico and conquering the Tour Divide.

Konan has accomplished more than most people would ever dream of attempting. However, my favorite thing about him is not his many accomplishments but who he is as a person. From the time he was a little kid, even when he lost, he's always kept a good attitude. And it's that same relentless positivity that draws people to him like a magnet. He has a God-given ability to inspire those around him, unlike anybody else that I've ever seen before. If you spend just a few hours with Konan, I guarantee that you'll leave feeling encouraged and uplifted.

That's why this book is so powerful. Through Konan's stories of adventure and what he's learned along the way, he'll genuinely make you believe that your impossible dreams are possible. He'll not only encourage you into taking your first step, but he'll coach you along the way as you reach heights you've never traveled before. If I've learned anything from my son, it's that anything is possible. Yes—I'm talking about your life, too! It starts with belief, and this book will help you do just that. If you want more out of life, read this book from the front cover to the back. It's time to GO and live your adventure!

INTRODUCTION
EXPERIENCES THAT SHAPE YOU

Sharp pain jolted my chest that shocked my entire body. There was no doubt in my mind that I was experiencing a heart attack. The whole thing made no sense to me: I was a collegiate athlete, long-distance runner, and in the best shape of my life. What in the world was going on with me?

This all happened on a Friday evening while I was on my way to the cafeteria. I was on a small grant to run cross country and track at Malone University—one of the most prestigious running schools in the area. I'd only been on campus for a few weeks as preseason training for the cross country team had just begun. On the first day of practice, all the runners have to run ten miles in under one hour to make the team. It wasn't an easy task, but I clocked in at under an hour and was given my official Malone jersey. For the next few weeks, I trained with my new teammates, some of which were world-class athletes. Everything was going smoothly. That's why these unexpected, excruciating chest pains made no sense to me whatsoever.

At nineteen years old, we all think we're pretty much invincible, and I was definitely no exception! I laid in bed for the entire weekend instead of going to the emergency room. Zero part of me had any interest in going for a ride in the ambulance, staying overnight at the hospital, or paying a massive medical bill. At the time my parents didn't have health insurance, so injuries would only be covered through the school. I decided to tough it out for the weekend until I could get into the nurse's office at Malone on Monday morning. I couldn't walk, roll over in bed, or take deep breaths.

Long story short, the school nurse examined me and panicked upon realizing my lung had partially collapsed. She frantically scurried to call the squad, and was shocked when I told her that I'd prefer to drive to the hospital myself. As the emergency room doctors gave me the synopsis, they let me know that there was no rhyme or reason as to why the injury occurred. It was simply something that happens to tall, slender athletes between the ages of eighteen and twenty-five from time to time. Just my luck!

The rehab process was extremely difficult for me physically, mentally, and emotionally. Running has been my passion since ninth grade. It all started while running bleachers at basketball practice one day. I was zooming up and down the steps, easily beating all of the other guys without really exerting too much energy. My basketball coach asked me if I had ever thought about running cross country. The first thing that crossed my mind was that he must have thought I was not a very good basketball player! He assured me that I had a natural ability for running. I joined the cross country team midseason and soon became the third best runner on the varsity team—and that was without the months of training that the other runners had gone through.

I was extremely competitive then, and honestly, not much has changed. The will to win has always driven me to push myself. When it came to running, I saw an opportunity to excel and possibly earn a college scholarship in the future. I decided to quit all other sports and make cross country and track my two main priorities. It was a decision that ended up paying off!

My favorite memory from my high school career is, without a doubt, running at the conference meet my senior year. The first event I participated in was the 4x800 relay, and our squad set the school record! After that, I won the mile. I was feeling pretty good and was taking a breather before competing in the two-mile race as well. That's when my coach approached me and started saying crazy things: "Konan, the two-mile starts in about fifteen minutes. Before that starts, I need you to compete in the half-mile. And by the way, for our school to have a chance at winning the track meet, you need to win the two-mile and at least place top-three in the half-mile."

Exhausted, I chugged some water and made my way over to the starting blocks. Although the half-mile wasn't my race, I ended up finishing in second place. Afterward—thank God—there was enough left in my tank to win the two-mile. My dad was there and literally ran the final stretch of the two-mile in front of the bleachers with me. He cheered for me at the top of his lungs the entire time. The crowd started clapping and cheering; I think more for him than me! I was chosen as the conference meet MVP. It was a moment I will never forget.

I was blessed to have two great distance coaches during high school in Paul Talkington and Jerry Fresenko. Both were All-Americans in college and my dream was to become one as well. That's why getting a small grant to run at Malone University was such a huge deal to me. The coach, Jack Hazen, was a legend, and running for him was going to be my big shot. Being a part of Malone's distance team was an opportunity to run alongside All- American athletes and learn from a world-class coach. It was a dream come true.

That's why the injury was so devastating. Not only had my lung collapsed, but it felt like my dream had collapsed right along with it. I worked my tail off during rehab but I was never the same after that. As a sophomore in college, I couldn't even run the same times that I did as a sophomore in high school. I had no answers and neither did the doctors. Eventually, I ended up transferring to another school and quit running altogether.

For the next five years, I still was active in other sports, but I hung up the running shoes. It was a season where I felt like I had lost a part of me. Up to this point, a good part of my life had revolved around running. Growing up, I was the kid who would come home from hanging at my friend's house at midnight, lace up my running shoes, and head out in the darkness to get my miles in. All of a sudden, that was stripped away from me, and it felt like a part of me was missing.

After about five years of not running, my brother Josh suggested that we run a sprint duathlon. For those of you who might not know, a sprint duathlon is a race that consists of a 5K run, 12-mile bike ride, and another 5K run. This was exactly the jolt I needed to get out of my funk. As I started to train again, my competitive juices started to flow again. On race day, I found out that my brother hadn't trained a lick, but it gave me the jump start I needed. I won my age group and found joy again in my running.

Winning that race gave me the competition bug again. I became determined to answer the question: *How far can I go?* Obviously, the only way to answer that question accurately was by testing my limits. I began searching for 5K's that I could compete in almost every weekend. In full transparency, I'd search out the races that had the slowest winners the year before, which helped me accumulate quite a few trophies and gift cards to eat just as many celebratory steak dinners. Next, I ran a half-marathon, which is a 13.1 mile run. After the half-marathon, I went straight to competing in the Iron Man Triathlon: a singular race that consists of a 2.4-mile swim, 112-mile bike ride, and 26.2-mile run. That one about killed me! However, it also developed a passion deep inside of me to continually push my limits.

Looking back, I'm so thankful that my brother asked me to run that sprint duathlon so long ago. Who knows where I'd be today if he hadn't. The truth is, regardless of who we are, we all have moments of difficulty. For me, it was a collapsed lung. Maybe you feel as if some of your dreams, goals, relationships, and sources of joy have collapsed too. Those are the moments when discouragement tries to tell us we're no longer allowed to thrive—just survive.

My hope is that this book helps to get you out of *surviving mode* and back into *thriving mode*. At the time of my injury, I never thought I'd compete again. But upon writing this book, I have been blessed to compete in some of the most grueling, sometimes dangerous, and incredibly physical challenges that this world has to offer. Through the process, I've discovered that there are really only two ways of approaching life: apathetically or adventurously.

The truth is, we're all hardwired for adventure. Think about it. When we were little kids, nobody had to teach us how to use our imaginations, how to dream, or even how to get into a little bit of trouble while testing our limits. Whether climbing trees, jumping our bike off a ramp, or using a rope swing, we used to live with such excitement, passion, and zeal! So the question becomes, *what happened to us?* For me, my passion never left, it was simply buried. I believe the same is true for you. And in the same way that sprint duathlon restored my desire to live adventurously once again, I hope that this book sparks a sense of adventure in you!

LIFE-ALTERING EXPERIENCES

I'm a big believer that our lives are shaped by two main things: relationships and experiences. Our parents, siblings, friends, spouses, teachers, and coaches are all relationships that shape us. Some of our relationships we can choose, while others we can't. When we think about our experiences, a lot of them are outside of our control. For example, you might have parents who got divorced when you were a kid. That was an experience you didn't have any control over but it certainly played a role in your development. Maybe you have lost your job because of a cutback, another experience that you have no control over. For many people, experiences outside of their control end up becoming what defines them. And trust me, I'm not trying to make light of the difficulty you've been through or the effect it's had on you. But take a minute to look at it in a different light.

While there are experiences we can't control, there are also ones that we can. You can control how hard you study, work, or train for something important to you. Applying to your dream college, or dream job, or trying out to be a part of a team is something you have control over. We also control how we allow each experience to shape us. We can actually choose experiences that will stretch us, shape us and challenge us—ones that will help grow us into stronger, more compassionate, and better people. All of this is within our control.

We must also realize, it's not just about the experience of what happens to us, but it's about how we choose to interpret it. **Sometimes we put so much emphasis on what happens *TO* us that we don't realize the important thing is what happens *IN* us.** Experiences have the power to shape us powerfully. So what would our lives look like if we chose to become intentional about our experiences? Not only intentional about planning experiences, but also choosing how we will be shaped by the experiences we can't control.

Here's what I believe: We can either wait for experiences to come to us, or we can intentionally pursue experiences that will shape us into who we want to become.

Difficulty is inevitable in life. But have you ever noticed that two people can come out of the exact same hardship looking completely different? While one person is crushed by it, the other uses it as a platform to thrive. The difference is that **we all *go through things* but we don't all *grow through things*.** The person who came out as a victim went through it, but the person who came out as a victor grew through it.

You have what it takes to grow! But you might be wondering: *How do I go about it?* I'm glad you asked!

First, change the way you look at the negative experiences you've been through. Some of you have experienced divorce, sickness, job loss, or the death of a family member. Those things hurt, and there's no way around that. But it's important to move forward and not stay hurt forever. What if we started looking at our difficulties as *forced-growth* opportunities to become overcomers? Instead of becoming bitter, we'd become better!

Secondly, we have to start choosing positive experiences rather than only being held hostage by negative ones. We must become intentional about what I call *living your adventure*. What would happen if you allowed yourself to dream again in the direction of your passion? I bet at the end of your life you'd look back and be pretty satisfied with the story that you wrote. The good news is that the pen is in your hand! You have permission to start writing your adventure and it starts right now!

Experts say that a child is only born with two fears: the fear of loud noises and the fear of falling. If that is true, that means every single other fear that haunts us has been learned. We've all been faced with fears that we have picked up somewhere. Unfortunately, because of those fears, we usually create a box with walls of fear and comfort. We think that if we can stay away from things that make us afraid or uncomfortable, nothing bad will happen. But if you've lived long enough, you know that bad things can happen either way. And as long as we're living inside of our boxes of fear and comfort, we'll never get to live the adventure that our souls so desperately desire.

It's time to step out of the box. It's time to stop allowing past experiences to define our lives and start defining our lives by choosing our experiences.

MEET YOUR ADVENTURE GUIDE

Just like you, I have anxieties and emotions that sometimes get the better of me. I'm definitely not an expert on living my adventure, but I would say I have some experience. For more than a decade, I've decided to become extremely intentional about my experiences. I've made the commitment to approach life in such a way to live it to the fullest. Up to this point, here are some of the major adventures I've completed:

- Competing in two Ironman distance triathlons
- Running the Boston Marathon
- Hiking the Benton Mackaye Trail (100 miles; 5 days)
- Hiking the Knobstone Trail (60 miles; 3 days)
- Swimming Alcatraz
- Kayaking the River Quest in the Yukon (444 miles)
- Running two 50K's (one in Zion, Utah)
- Running a 50-mile ultra marathon

- Running a 100-mile ultra marathon
- Biking the Tour the Divide (Canada to Mexico; off-road and unsupported)
- Running rim to rim to rim at the Grand Canyon
- Climbing Mount Kilimanjaro in two days (two half-days and one full-day)

It's easy to look at that list and think that I'm some sort of physical specimen or guru on mental toughness. But trust me, neither of those is true! Many of my adventures have stretched me beyond my limits. And yes, some of them have even made me want to cry! But the one thing I always made sure to do along the way was to learn from the experience.

For the rest of this book, I will be sharing stories from the biggest adventures and challenges of my life. Along the way, I'm going to share what I've learned from my experiences. One thing I've learned is every adventure goes better with a guide—someone who knows how to navigate the path you're traveling. From this point forward, consider me your own personal adventure guide. Every chapter, I'll leave you with an Adventure Guide Tip that you can apply to your own personal adventure in life.

I know that not everyone reading will want, or is crazy enough, to run 100 miles or climb Mount Kilimanjaro. But regardless of who you are, you were built for some sort of adventure. It might be the adventure of taking up a new hobby, going back to school, losing weight, overcoming addiction, or starting a new business. Whatever it is, there's a path of excitement and fulfillment out there waiting for you. Let's learn how to go live your adventure!!

ADVENTURE #1

100-MILE ULTRA

CHAPTER 1

TRAINING LIKE A CHAMPION

For the next few chapters, I want to share some stories about my experience running a 100-mile ultramarathon. And yes, you most likely processed the details of the adventure correctly upon reading its name. A 100-mile ultra is a 100-mile race that you run on foot. Typically, it starts around 4:00 a.m. and doesn't stop until you cross the finish line. To give you an idea of how long it takes to complete, most ultra locations have a cutoff time of about thirty hours, depending on the difficulty of the course. The course that I ran was the Burning River in Cuyahoga Falls, Ohio.

You might be wondering: *What possesses someone to run for a day straight with very few breaks?* Admittedly, that's not something that sounds appealing to the average person. For me, it didn't take much. I was relaxing at home one day, flipping through a magazine, when an ad on one of the pages caught my eye. It was a picture of a cowboy-looking dude wearing a huge, brass belt buckle that displayed a 100-mile icon. Underneath Cowboy Man was a phrase that captivated me: "You are stronger than you think you are...100-mile race."

The idea of running 100 miles hit me like a ton of bricks. It was hard for me to fathom what a race like that would be like. I tried to imagine myself conquering a challenge of that magnitude: waking up to train every day, running through the sunrise and sunset, and pushing myself to the brink of exhaustion. Oddly enough, I was sold! A few days later, I registered to run my first 100-mile ultra marathon. No turning back.

Before I started training, the farthest that I had ever run was 26.2 miles, which is a standard marathon. The length of the ultra would be nearly four times that distance. In their current state, my body, mind, and emotions were not prepared for that type of challenge. That meant unless I got serious about the preparation this type of race requires, I wouldn't even come close to finishing. I took a few days to search training plans on the internet, picked out the one that suited me best, and got straight to work.

Training for this type of race consumed a considerable amount of my time. In fact, it almost felt like I picked up a part-time job for six months. During weekdays, my runs were usually anywhere between eight to fifteen miles in distance. On the weekends, they were typically closer to twenty to thirty miles. Because of the level of commitment the training would require, I got my family to sign-off and approve my schedule. I made two promises to them: during the week I'd run before work and on the weekends I'd be back by lunch. This meant that on my long-distance days my alarm would go off at 3:30 a.m. to run. Sometimes, I'd train for up to four or five hours, hop in the shower, take a ten-minute nap, and head off to work. Talk about some long days!

On top of the time that the training ate up, it also required a great deal of intentionality when it came to planning. Every day, I had to check the suggested mileage from the training plan and adjust my schedule accordingly. On top of that, I had a group of guys that agreed to help me train. On long run days, they'd alternate and run portions of the mileage with me. For example, one would run the first ten miles with me, while another might jump in for the next eight, and yet another would help me grind out the last five.

In all honesty, I needed accountability. Knowing that a friend was going out of his way to wake up at 3:30 in the morning to help me forced me to get out of bed when I didn't feel like it.

On top of all this, I had to eat like a racehorse. It seemed like every hour my body needed to be refueled with carbohydrates, protein, and hydration. I suppose one perk of training so hard was the countless number of guilt-free PB&J sandwiches! But if I slacked on my nutrition at all, I wouldn't have the energy for training, work, or my family.

In full transparency, there were so many times that I didn't feel like waking up when my alarm went off. In fact, if I documented all of the times I wanted to skip training, it would probably be enough content for this entire book. The mattress feels extra comfy and the sheets seem extra warm when you're craving sleep. I have learned there are two pains in life: the pain of discipline and the pain of regret. And the pain of discipline has a way better return on investment! So time after time, I rolled out of bed, laced up my shoes, and hit the trails.

There were mornings when the temperature was in single digits before the sun came up. Icicles literally formed on my eyelashes multiple times! Other times, I was traveling for work and found myself running unknown routes, hoping that I would remember how to make it back to the hotel. Probably my favorite training story was my experience of running in a foreign country. I went on a mission trip with my church, and because the surrounding area was dangerous, I couldn't leave the compound to run. It was the perfect excuse to skip training! But instead of missing, I chose to run-in-place inside the walls of a ten-by-ten-foot courtyard for an hour or more. Talk about boring scenery!

You might be wondering: *Konan, why were you so intense about your training?* Truthfully, it's not because I *wanted* to be, it's because I *had* to be. If I had allowed myself to slack on my training, I would have fallen short of my 100-mile goal on the day of the ultra. You can't just wake up one day, grit your teeth, and run that kind of distance. I couldn't afford to be unintentional. When it comes to our goals, a lack of preparation always leads to the frustration of falling short of the finish line.

It's the difference between *joggers* and *runners*. Joggers train when it's nice outside while runners train regardless. Former Oregon Coach Bill Boweman said, "There is no such thing as rough weather, just soft people." In other words, runners don't abandon their plan when it's not opportunistic. They're intentional about their preparation even in the face of obstacles. In the same way, our adventures in life require intentional training—when it's sunny, but also when it's sleeting.

ADVENTURE GUIDE TIP

Looking back, the 100-mile ultra was maybe the most accomplished twenty-eight hours of my life. However, the physical and mental training that made those twenty-eight hours possible required much, much more of me than the race itself. That's the way life works: **accomplishment never happens without investment.** The ultra required some incredible investment. This leads perfectly to our Adventure Guide Tip:

THE BIGGER THE GOAL, THE HARDER AND MORE DISCIPLINED YOU MUST TRAIN.

From my experience, I've found that training always requires two things: hunger and discipline. Hunger is what I refer to as the *fire in your belly.* In order to accomplish anything in life, we must be hungry for it. The very thought of it has to create a fire, or passion, deep inside of us. But while hunger is important, if it's all you have, you'll only train sporadically instead of consistently. If training is ever going to become a regular part of your life, hunger must be paired with discipline. Discipline is *doing what you don't want to do in order to get what you've always wanted.* In other words, there will be times when you don't feel like training, regardless of what you're preparing for. Trust me, I get it. In those moments, it's important to lean on discipline to get you through.

Most people don't care to run 100-mile races in their lifetime. Maybe you're into that type of thing or maybe you're wired for a different type of stretching experience. Regardless of what your adventure looks like, it will likely require some form of training and preparation. It would be nice to simply show up, have fun, and kick butt at all of life's adventures. But unfortunately, that dream is unrealistic. Trust me, if I would have just *shown up* to the Ultra, it would have eaten me for breakfast. And I would have been pretty embarrassed in the process. It's the same way with you. There are two major areas in life that I've found require training:

1. Opportunities outside of your comfort zone.

One way to define an adventure is *an opportunity outside of your comfort zone.* When you're given the chance to pursue something that isn't natural for you, or is outside the scope of your current ability, you'll be forced to choose whether or not you're willing to leave your comfort zone. Why? Because anything that falls within your comfort zone doesn't require adventurous ambition. Those types of opportunities don't make your heart race and your palms sweat when you think about them. They don't take much extra exertion or energy to achieve. You can just roll out of bed and make them happen without thinking too much about it.

Opportunities that fall outside of your comfort zone are different. They force you to contemplate your limits and make you wonder if you actually have what it takes. You know that in order to achieve them, some type of growth will be necessary: physical, mental, emotional, spiritual, or maybe even all of the above! Outside of your comfort zone is where an adventurous attitude is required. Only people who are willing to be vulnerable, grit their teeth, and display commitment will do well in this territory.

Opportunities outside of your comfort zone attempt to push you to heights that you've never before reached. That means in order to get there, some type of training will be necessary. The farther into the unknown you're looking to travel, the more training you'll need to complete to get there.

For me, the opportunity that screamed through an ad in a random magazine was to run 100 miles. Maybe you're looking to accomplish something similar, or possibly a different type of adventure has your name written on it. All of our comfort zones are different according to our natural abilities and personalities. But here are a few adventures that might require some type of training in our lives: walking three miles a day, running a 5K, building fifteen pounds of muscle, starting a business or side-hustle, becoming a leader, writing a book, getting out of debt, or investing your money.

What opportunity outside of your comfort zone has been challenging you to conquer it? With the right training, you can expand the walls of your fears and comfort zone to accomplish things you previously thought to be impossible.

2. The things that matter the most.

Often, we invest the same amount of our energy into the things that matter the most to us as we do with the things that matter the least. There are probably many reasons why we do so: a lack of gratitude, busyness, depleted energy, and the countless distractions in our lives are a few that come to mind. However, when you think about it, this way of living keeps us out of *thriving* and makes us prisoners to *surviving*.

The areas that should matter the most to you are the ones that add the most value to your life. They are the people you love, the relationships that enrich you, and the ways you can make the lives of those around you better. These are the things, above anything else, that you should train for the most. Think about it for a second! Marriage is the relationship that shapes your life more than anything else. However, most people never train for it. They don't go to premarital counseling or attend marriage conferences, and even avoid date nights. Likewise, parents have the opportunity to deeply influence the lives of their children and mold them into who they will become. And while a lot of parents do a great job of loving their kids, many of them don't ever read books, take classes, or learn from mentors about raising their kids. It's the same with mental health. Most people never deal with their deep hurts and issues, even when fear, anxiety, or worry consumes their lives. The list goes on and on!

While opportunities outside of our comfort zones are adventures, I also believe that our lives can be lived as adventures. What do I mean by that? Our relationships, jobs, and passions can bring us fresh and exciting experiences every single day! But as long as we just *wing it* when it comes to things like marriage, parenting, and our careers, our daily experiences will remain mundane and unfulfilling. We will become stagnant in most areas of our lives while never growing, achieving, or accomplishing anything.

Here are a couple questions that I have for you: What areas of your life matter the most to you? Do you have a training plan in place for those areas? Although training can be difficult, I can guarantee you that it's also worth it. Not only will you thank yourself in the long run, the people who matter the most to you will thank you as well.

ADVENTURE APPLICATION

1. Throughout the course of your life, what things have you trained for? Did that training pay off and how so?

2. According to our definition of discipline—doing what you don't want to do in order to get what you've always wanted—would you consider yourself a disciplined person? How might you be able to improve in the area of discipline?

3. Do you intentionally train for opportunities outside of your comfort zone and the things in life that matter the most to you? If not, get started by developing a plan for one area of your life!

CHAPTER 2
STRIDING THROUGH THE SUCK

The night before the ultra provided one of the worst rounds of sleep that I'd had in a while. It was similar to having jitters the night before the first day of school or a big championship game. The competitor inside of me was so hyped up that I woke up ready to run through a wall just about every hour.

Looking back, my restlessness probably turned out to be a good thing because it gave me an opportunity to eat—a lot! Your body sheds so many calories running for twenty-eight hours straight that it's important to start out with as much food and water in your stomach as physically possible. Right before bed, I scarfed down one of the largest meals you'd ever seen and washed it down by chugging water until my stomach said to stop. When I woke up at one o'clock in the morning, I did the same thing again. And finally, at three o'clock in the morning, I repeated the process one more time. It didn't feel great in the moment, but I knew that my body would thank me for the fuel during the race.

Finally, 4:00 a.m. rolled around, and it was time to start the race. It was still pitch-black dark with the only light coming from the headlamps that all of the runners were wearing. I vividly remember the thoughts and emotions I experienced waiting for the ultra to start. It's a pretty surreal feeling knowing that you're about to push yourself to your absolute limit by running 100 miles straight. It's hard to fully explain, but a cocktail of adrenaline, nervousness, excitement, and fear ran through me. All of the emotions stirred up and settled in my stomach, leaving me with some pretty intense butterflies.

In the minutes before the race, I attempted to look upon the course I'd be running in just a few minutes. My head lamp was dull and I could only see about 100 feet ahead of me at best. In other words, I was about to run 100 miles but could only get eyes on a tiny fraction of that distance. It was in that moment that I realized I was about to embark upon a huge unknown.

Unknowns are polarizing and everybody responds to them differently. From my observation, most people end up freaked out and gripped by fear when they can't fully grasp what they're up against. However, I've found that there is another way to view things. We often assume that whatever is behind an unknown door is automatically bad. But what if we opened up the door to find something really great? Optimism is the ability to look at life's unknowns as exciting opportunities! An adventurous life requires us to approach challenges with a glass half-full type of attitude. Without it, we'll never open the door. And without opening the door, we'll never discover what can be possible by doing so.

Honestly, as I stared at the greatest unknown I'd ever faced, I felt torn. A friend had asked me if I was excited before the race. In a moment of self-evaluation, I let them know that I was both excited and nervous. Then they asked me a follow-up question that pierced my heart and opened my eyes: *Konan, what are you afraid of?*

That simple question forced me to be honest with myself. Like most people, I had a deep-rooted fear of failure. I had conquered a lot of other adventures, and that's what the people in my life had come to expect from me. But this one was different. I truly did not know if I had what it takes to run 100 miles. And to make matters worse, a lot of people knew that I was competing in the ultra. Heck, most of my family, friends, and employees would be following the race! There was no such thing as private results for me, only public ones. I knew that this would either be my greatest physical feat or greatest failure to date.

Finally, the gun went off and the race began. The last thing that you want to do is take off too fast and burn all of your energy at the beginning. During the first few miles, it felt as if a huge weight had been removed from my chest. It felt good to be running at a nice, steady pace, but felt even better to finally get going. Maybe this will be an encouragement for someone: When anticipation and anxiety build around an unknown adventure, sometimes the best thing that you can do is just dive in head first. Once I started the ultra, there was no turning back. Once I was in it, I was forced to give it my best shot. When it comes to life's unknowns, the best thing we can do is leave the sidelines, get in the game, and do the best we can possibly do.

Trying to mentally process an ultra is a unique adventure in itself. I cruised through the first twenty miles and felt great. After mile twenty-six, I thought: *Wow! I just ran an entire marathon and I am still only a quarter of the way through.* However, I was determined and continued to press on.

At about mile forty, I stopped at an aid station to rehydrate, eat, and rest for a few minutes. Thankfully, some family and friends were waiting for me there, which was a needed boost to my morale. At this point in the race, my stomach was bloating slightly, but my overall energy was good. I accepted my crew's offer to roll out my leg muscles, thinking it could only help. In retrospect, it turned out to be a pretty big mistake.

The leg roller got my lactic acid moving around. Because my stomach was already bloated, stirred up lactic acid was the last thing that I needed. When I hit mile forty-four, I knew with 100-percent certainty that I was going to be sick. Do you remember all of the food that I ate the night before? Me too! Unfortunately, I got to taste it all twice; once when it went down, and again when it came back up. I sat down on a log and vomited profusely. I was sweating bullets, my body ached, and my stomach was in knots.

In that moment, I was once again forced to face my fear of failure. But this time was different. Before the race, I hoped that I wouldn't fail. Now as I was puking my guts out, failure seemed inevitable. To make matters worse, I hadn't even made it to the halfway marker yet. So many doubts began to run through my head: *Am I still able to run? Is my dream over? What am I going to tell my family? What am I going to tell my friends?*

As I wallowed in my self-pity, a man with an Airborne Ranger tattoo on his calf ran up to me. He had a tough looking exterior and deep, gruff voice.

"Hey," he yelled like a drill sergeant. "You alright?"

"Duuude, I've been tossing my cookies all over the place," I responded.

"Let me give you a little tip," he said as he ran past and looked back at me. "You can sit there and throw up, or you can walk and throw up. But I promise you that if you sit there, you might as well throw in the towel because your race will be over. Get up!"

As a full-grown man, it had been a while since I'd been challenged like that. But in a strange way, it was exactly the encouragement I needed to hear. I stood up while my stomach was still in knots. Slowly but surely, I put one foot in front of the other and started walking. I made it a few feet, bent over, and threw up again. But I was determined to keep going. Like an inspirational scene from a movie, I wiped the vomit from my face, put one foot in front of the other, and pressed on. Pretty soon a walk turned into a jog. Before long, I caught the Airborne Ranger and thanked him for some of the best advice I'd ever received. The only thing he said was, "Way to go, guy. Finish the race!"

Before I knew it, I was back on pace. All because I chose to keep walking when the going got tough.

ADVENTURE GUIDE TIP

When it comes to running an ultra, a lot of people have given up while throwing up. It's tough to physically and mentally bounce back in a race like that. Truthfully, it would have been easy to quit while sitting on that log. If I had, it would have been a decision made in a moment of defeat that I'd have to live with for the rest of my life. If it wasn't for the advice of the Airborne Ranger, who knows what would have happened. The Adventure Guide Tip for this chapter was a game-changer for me in that moment, and I believe it can be a game-changer for you in your moment:

YOU CAN SIT THERE AND THROW UP, OR YOU CAN WALK AND THROW UP.

Let me rephrase my friend's point differently so, hopefully, it can resonate with you. When we live our adventures, tough moments are inevitable. **Sometimes, things are just going to suck! However, we get to choose whether or not we keep our stride in the middle of *the suck*.** Sometimes, as I was prepared to do on the log, we settle for just sitting there during difficult situations. The ironic thing is that it's going to suck either way. All of us know that throwing up is painful whether we are sitting down or standing up. If *the suck* is inevitable, we might as well stand up tall, take the hit, keep our stride, and continue to move forward.

I'm sure that you can think of a person or two in your life that, after things got messy, decided it was just easier to stay put. The truth is, it probably *is* easier to sit on your metaphorical log and wallow in self-pity. But here's a bit of encouragement: In the long run, you'll be so much happier that you chose to walk instead of wallow. The accomplishment of goals, the fulfillment of dreams, and the excitement of adventure are impossible for sitters, but possible for walkers.

I want to be honest with you: living this way will require resiliency. One of the most resilient men that I've ever read about is Winston Churchill. In fact, there's a lot that we can learn from him.

The sixty-five-year-old Churchill was elected as Great Britain's Prime Minister in 1940. Around that same time, Great Britain looked to be doomed in World War. France, their allies, had been knocked out of the war, Nazi Germany controlled all of Europe, and the British troops found themselves scrambling to survive. When it looked as if the only reasonable move remaining was to surrender, Churchill stayed resilient, even saying that surrendering was something he'd never do. As a rally cry to his nation, Churchill is credited with saying this famous quote: "If you're going through hell, keep going."[1]

With the help of other allies, Great Britain held on and eventually became victorious against Nazi Germany. Why? Because when they had to walk through hell, they chose to keep walking. In other words, they made the commitment to walk and throw up instead of sit and throw up.

My heart is not to downplay your difficulties, but I do want to challenge you to keep walking through them. I'm not even saying that you need to conjure up the strength to run through them. But there are so many areas of life where we can simply choose to put one foot in front of the other and keep walking.

- Maybe your marriage has hit some speed bumps. Keep working on it!
- Maybe you're having a tough time getting through to your kids. Keep putting forth effort!
- Maybe you've got a particularly tough academic semester ahead of you. Keep studying!
- Maybe you haven't heard back from any of the jobs you've applied for. Keep applying!
- Maybe you didn't make the team last year. Keep practicing!
- Maybe you didn't finish the half-marathon. Keep training!

The great Martin Luther King Jr. said it like this: "If you can't fly, run; if you can't run, walk; if you can't walk, crawl; but by all means keep moving forward."[2] Whatever you do, keep moving forward. Your adventure, your dreams, and your future all depend on you putting one foot in front of the other.

ADVENTURE APPLICATION

1. When things get hard, do you usually stop or do you continue to move forward? Why?

2. What's one thing you've given up on that you're challenged to pick up again?

CHAPTER 3
FRIENDS WHO FIGHT
WITH YOU

If it wasn't for some great friends, I'm not sure that I would have accomplished my goal of finishing the ultra. Because 100 miles is such a long distance to run, the race officials allow you to run with pacers. For those who might not know, pacers are an individual or team of runners you select to run portions of the race alongside you. Their job is to help you run at a consistent pace: speeding you up, slowing you down, and encouraging you as needed. My pacing crew consisted of some great friends whose names were Denny, Jason, and Herb.

I'm so thankful for how committed they were to our friendship, not just during the race, but throughout the entire process. I mentioned this in chapter one, but these guys trained with me. They provided much needed accountability on the days I didn't feel like rolling out of bed. But even more so, they were much needed accountability during some of my lowest moments of the race.

The cool thing about our team was that we all ran the furthest distance we ever had on the day of the race. I obviously ran the full hundred miles. But Denny ran about fifty-six miles while Jason and Herb both ran close to the length of a marathon. In other words, we all set personal records that day! There's something special about conquering a challenge with your friends. Maybe you've been on a team—playing sports, at work, or volunteering—where you've experienced a special kind of adventure with others. It has a way of cementing your friendship and bonding you together for a lifetime. This was the case with our running group, because trust me, we conquered some pretty demanding challenges that day.

Denny ran the first fifty-six miles of the ultra, which is quite a feat. About fifty miles into the race, Jason ran stride-by-stride with me for hours. He's a quiet guy, and honestly, we didn't say all that much during our time together. But that's the thing about friendship: it's just as important to be there for somebody as it is to have the perfect words. About the same time Jason finished running his marathon, Herb linked up with me to run the last quarter of the race. He was the closer, which turned out to be the toughest role of them all!

At mile seventy-five, I stopped at an aid station to refuel and rest for a few minutes. Once again, my crew asked me if I wanted my legs rolled. At that time, I was unaware of the sickening effect it was having on my body. I naively agreed, and moments later I found myself puking once again.

That moment turned out to be an extremely challenging one for me. I was completely gassed physically; I had been running non-stop since four in the morning. It's quite the experience to begin running before sunrise and continue running for long enough to see the sunset. On top of that, there was still the length of a full marathon left to run. The thoughts of doubt quickly returned. It was dark and I felt I was at the end of my rope. I remember in that moment realizing that I was writing my story that my kids would tell even after I was gone. At that exact moment, the pen was in my hand. So I got up, wiped the vomit from my face, and pressed on yet again.

During that last leg of the race, Herb got to witness me in an extremely compromised physical and mental state. He wasn't running with the Konan he had gotten to know so well over the past few months of training. My energy was low, my vocal cords didn't have enough strength to produce anything more than a whisper, and my brain function was foggy at best. In fact, things got so bad that I actually started to hallucinate. It was completely dark and we only had our headlamps to illuminate the night. We were running on a trail through the woods when the wind started to toss the leaves on the trees around. I could have sworn that a mountain lion or some type of gigantic cat ran across the trail right in front of us.

"Bro, was that a mountain lion?!" I said with some panic in my voice.

"Konan, you are hallucinating. Everything is completely fine," Herb replied with a chuckle.

To this day, the idea that a mountain lion ran across our path still feels real to me, even though it was undoubtedly a hallucination. I wish there was a way to know what I would have done if Herb wasn't there to talk some sense into me.

In that moment, I realized the importance of having friends who will speak the truth to you. Throughout the adventure of life, there will be moments when we are compromised physically, mentally, emotionally, and spiritually. Every single one of us has experienced a season when it's hard to keep our head on straight. During those moments, we tend to see through a lens of pain, discomfort, and hurt rather than a lens of reality. Sometimes, we create a negative outlook about our schools, jobs, or futures simply because we're looking through the wrong lens. In the same vein, it's easy to assume that people are saying or thinking the worst about you, even though that may be the furthest thing from the truth. In difficult moments, we often hallucinate, creating realities that aren't actually true.

In those moments, we all need a Herb in our life who will help us differentiate fear from reality. We need friends who will speak the truth to us when we're having a hard time seeing or believing.

ADVENTURE GUIDE TIP

I can't take credit for this Adventure Guide Tip. It's only appropriate to give the nod to my running team: Denny, Jason, and Herb. They taught me so much, including the following lesson:

WHEN THE GOING GETS TOUGH, YOU NEED TOUGH FRIENDS.

When you run a hundred mile race, it's full of ups and downs. At one moment you feel like you could run forever, and the next you're hallucinating. The greater the distance, the more your weaknesses are exposed. It's pretty similar to the way life works. One moment things are going great, and the next you feel like you're falling apart. The longer you live, the more you come face-to-face with your weakness.

Although vulnerability is healthy, most of us fight it tooth and nail. It's easier to keep our weaknesses to ourselves rather than share them with our closest friends and family, allowing them to share the load of our burdens. The great thing about the ultra is that I had no choice but to share my weakness with three of my friends. The farther I went, the weaker I became. Even if I had tried, there would have been no way to hide it from them. Looking back, I'm thankful that was the case. They were able to become a source of strength during my struggle only because my weakness was exposed. Even the best of friends can't help what we hide.

It's so important that we have tough friends when the going gets tough in our lives. It's also important to be that friend for a few other people. We all need someone who loves us enough to speak the truth when we've believed lies. People who will help us keep the pace when we're physically and emotionally spent are necessary, not only in adventurous living, but any type of quality living.

Here's another way to say it: **You need friends who are willing to sit in the dirt with you.** Throughout the course of the race, all three of my friends sat on the ground with me at aid stations, even though they had fresher legs and the energy to continue running. In other words, they slowed down to be with me. When I was struggling, they chose to sit in the struggle with me. I was more important to them than their own personal agendas.

There are some undeniable qualities that all three of my pacers possessed. Looking back, these qualities can be used to help you find the right type of friendships. Even more importantly, they can be used as goals for the type of friend you should aim to be. Here are some qualities that great friends possess:

- Great friends sit with you when there's nothing to say.
- Great friends don't abandon you even when staying is inconvenient for them.
- Great friends aren't afraid to get your mess on them.
- Great friends push themselves past their limits to see you succeed.
- Great friends speak the truth even when it's hard to hear.
- Great friends are positive when you're negative.
- Great friends face the dark of the night with you.

You might be looking at this list discouraged, thinking: *I really don't have any friendships like that.* Can I encourage you for a second? Those special types of bonds aren't developed overnight. In fact, I knew Denny, Jason, and Herb long before we ran the race together. And on top of that, we spent months training together leading up to the ultra. The best friendships take time to develop because trust isn't solidified overnight.

The best relationships are the ones built on the foundation of trust. However, trust requires vulnerability. If you don't have any close friends, maybe it's time to wisely evaluate who you'd be willing to share some of your mess with. I'm not saying that you need to trust them with *everything* right away, but I am saying that sometimes it means you have to take the first step. I've found that vulnerability is contagious. **The more that you become vulnerable with your friends, the more vulnerable your friends become with you.** Is vulnerability scary? Absolutely! But life-giving relationships are on the other side of stepping into that fear.

You've probably heard the statement: Show me your friends, and I'll show you your future. I've found that to be 100-percent true. I believe that your future becomes brighter with great friends. It also becomes brighter when you choose to be a great friend! We weren't meant to live life alone, and we certainly don't have the ability to adventure alone. Your relationships matter. When the going gets tough, lean on your tough friends!

ADVENTURE APPLICATION

1. Think of a moment when someone sat in the dirt with you. How is your life different because of it? If you never have, reach out and tell them thank you!

2. Do you have great friends in your life? If not, of the people around you, who might be the right fit for a closer friendship?

3. Are you a great friend to anyone in your life? If not, how could you become a better one?

CHAPTER 4

SUFFERING PRODUCES

As we come to the last chapter about the ultra, let's talk about my experiences at the end of the race. You've probably heard the popular quote from author Jim George that reads: "It's not how you start that's important, but how you finish!" I've found this statement to hold true with every adventure in which I've ever participated. It certainly did with the ultra. It takes courage to start something, but just starting doesn't typically cost you much. Finishing, on the other hand, rarely comes at a discounted price. It will usually cost you more than you were planning on paying.

The last leg of the race felt dark—in more ways than one. First of all, it was dark outside. When you're completely spent, compromised visibility really takes a toll on you. In an ironic way, the physical darkness that surrounded me was an illustration of the state of my mind. It felt as if my mentality was fully engulfed by darkness.

The last twenty miles of the race was when my true grit was tested. All of the excitement of competing in a new adventure had worn off. The new car smell was completely gone. On top of that, my body felt depleted of the physical energy required to continue. I'm naturally a pretty skinny guy, which means that I don't have much fat to burn. After running seventy-five miles, my body had already consumed the little bit of fat that I did have and I was left feeling completely hollow.

We've all been tired before. The fatigue I felt in that moment was more than just needing a good night's sleep. It was complete and total exhaustion. My body was running on empty. As I thought about running the last twenty or so miles, it felt like I was preparing to run another hundred. If I was going to finish, it was guaranteed to be an intense mental battle.

As I did my best to push back against the darkness that settled over me, a weighty thought popped into my head: *Konan, at this very moment, you're writing the story about you that's going to be spoken forever.* A lot of times, we get so consumed with the difficulty of the present that we forget it will someday become our past. In other words, in every moment, we're writing the stories that we'll be able to tell in the future. The very ones that our loved ones will use to define us and pass on to future generations.

Right there, in the middle of the night, I began imagining the story that my children would tell my grandkids and great grandkids. What would they say about their dad?

If I gave up at that moment, the story they told might sound something like this: "Our dad was a pretty crazy guy. When we were teenagers, he competed in a one hundred mile race. He came close, but eventually gave up around mile eighty."

That obviously wasn't the story I wanted passed down from generation to generation within my family! I began to imagine how the narrative would change if I gutted out the last twenty miles: "Our dad was an extremely crazy guy. When we were teenagers, he not only competed in, but also completed a 100-mile race! He faced some tough challenges around mile eighty, but he pushed through and overcame them. One thing I learned from dad was determination—he always finished what he started."

Now that was the type of legacy I wanted to leave behind. And although I was exhausted, that very moment provided me with the opportunity to build that type of legacy. The pen was in my hand. I was writing the story that would be spoken over my life forever.

After what felt like an eternity, I reached mile ninety-nine. Of course, before crossing the finish line, runners had to run up a set of 100 steps to get out of the valley in which we'd been jogging for miles. Thanks to the course creators for putting the steps at the very end—the greatest point of exhaustion! But with burning calves, I reached the top of the steps and began pushing through the final mile.

The sun was now up as I battled the final stretch. Sunshine has a unique ability to renew life within you. Even though I was completely fried—physically, mentally, and emotionally—the sun birthed new hope inside of me. The last mile of the race led me into town where friends and family were lining the street to cheer runners on as they finished the last leg. It was during that stretch that it finally hit me: I was going to finish a 100-mile race.

Crossing the finish line was extremely emotional for me. If you ever hang out and observe the end of a long race, you'll often witness competitors break down and cry after running past the finish line. It's possible that a few tears ran down my cheeks, as well!

The difficulty of running for twenty-eight hours straight was overwhelming on many levels. I had picked a fight with my own limitations and came out victorious. But it was even more than that: for the past six months I had planned, trained, and sacrificed. I pushed myself through injuries, even when I wasn't sure if it was good for me. I went through my days exhausted as the lack of sleep and training had wiped out my energy.

The sacrifice that the ultra required made crossing the finish line so much more rewarding. The greatest accomplishment of any adventure is not the accolades that come with achievement. Adventure pushes us to our own limits. It forces us to figure out who we really are and what we really have deep inside of us. Adventure's greatest purpose is to develop us as people.

ADVENTURE GUIDE TIP

Everybody has a picture of who they'd like to become someday. Maybe you envision yourself as somebody who's unbelievably kind and generous to everyone that you meet. Or perhaps your goal is to become someone who chases after all your dreams. You might desire to be the most loving spouse, parent, or grandparent you can be. We all have a vision of what the best version of ourselves would look like. Although there are differences in the people we envision ourselves becoming, the path to becoming that person looks very similar for everyone.

I hate to break this to you, but change requires us to face some tough stuff. I know, I know! That's something that nobody gets excited about, including myself. But hear me out for a second: Have you ever noticed that our lives undergo the most transformation when we're in the middle of tough seasons? The tough stuff has a way of producing results that easy things never could. We all naturally desire every season to be comfortable and have thriving relationships without any challenges to face along the way. And while those seasons are nice, they don't do much for our development. Challenges change us. Frustrations form us. Misery molds us.

All of this might be tough to hear, but sometimes the hard truth is the most powerful truth. This Adventure Guide Tip is a hard truth, but a good one. Here it goes:

SUFFERING SHAPES OUR STORIES.

During the last leg of the ultra, I realized that the pen was in my hand and I could write whatever story I wanted to be told in the future. However, that story came at a cost. I had to push through extreme exhaustion, my body shutting down, and crippling doubt. It's easy to get excited when we hear a phrase like: *You can write whatever story you want!* Unfortunately, the pen that writes the story is suffering. To ink the ending that we want, we must endure.

Suffering shapes our stories in ways that comfort never could. The experience of the ultra combined with other things I've gone through in my life have taught me three major things that suffering produces in our lives:

1. Suffering produces humility.

Most of us would like to believe that we're superhuman because it's much easier than being vulnerable. For some reason, it seems as if there's something hardwired inside of us that doesn't like to admit weakness. However, the longer you live, the more life brings your weaknesses to the surface. Why? Because we're all human, and weakness is synonymous with our humanity.

Physical challenges have a unique ability to draw out our weakness quicker than almost anything else. I'd say the same thing about nature. As people, we are limited. Physical challenges, especially when outdoors in the elements, are not respecters of those limits. The ultra didn't care that my running muscles were being stretched two times past their previous capacity. The sun didn't take my preference to run during the daytime into consideration when it set at night. The 100 stairs at mile ninety-nine didn't seem to mind that my legs were already burning like never before. These things revealed my weakness, and my weakness produced humility.

Here's how I define humility: Understanding who you are and where you are in the vast scheme of things. We naturally want to elevate ourselves above others, or sometimes believe that we're bigger than we actually are. But do you know what's interesting? Right now, there are almost eight billion people alive in the world. That means that you are one of eight billion humans on the planet!

Humility isn't about minimizing yourself, but it is about realizing that you are a part of something bigger. It's necessary to become a person who values others, serves others, and uses their gifts to make an impact in the world. Regardless of what your adventure is, if it's going to make a difference in the lives of others, it requires humility.

2. Suffering produces growth.

Suffering has a way of tilling the ground of our lives for seeds of growth to be planted. What do I mean by this? When it comes to planting anything—a flower, vegetable, or tree—the potential for growth first lies within a seed. In order for a seed to grow, it must be planted. For it to be planted, the ground must be tilled, or dug up, by powerful machinery. If the ground had the capacity to feel, the tilling process would be a painful one.

In the same way, for our seeds of character and endurance to grow, our foundations must endure the painful process of tilling. Suffering shakes up the soil of our lives enough so that we have the capacity to grow. But let's take the whole thing a step further: When you plant a seed, the final product doesn't pop up right away. For example, a tomato doesn't start as a tomato. It starts as a seed and grows into a tomato. We don't automatically start as the people we want to become someday. Seeds are planted and then we grow to become those people. And it all starts with suffering.

We tend to avoid problems like the plague because we hate the suffering attached to them. But **every problem is an opportunity for growth.** This helps us to reframe the way we view difficulty. The problems you're facing in your marriage are an opportunity for you and your spouse to grow a deeper love for each other. Finals week may be stressful, but it is an opportunity to learn more than you ever have before. Your next game against that undefeated team is an opportunity to prove yourself against the best of the best. The loss of your job is an opportunity to reevaluate your passion. When we look at problems the right way, they can maximize growth in our lives.

3. Suffering produces gratitude.

In the middle of the suffering of the ultra, I tried my hardest to fight against thoughts of pessimism. After all, the ultra was an event that was on my bucket list! If I was going to do it, I wanted to enjoy it. Often, our biggest discouragements come attached to our biggest dreams. That's why it's important to maintain an attitude of gratitude.

In a strange way, the suffering almost made me more grateful. It sucked. But even just competing in the ultra is something that 99 percent of people will never do. I became grateful for the opportunity, the health to give it my best shot, and the friends and family who supported me. In the middle of suffering, I had a deep sense of gratitude.

In the same way, your deepest moments of suffering can produce your deepest levels of gratitude. Maybe when you look at this season, there are a million reasons to be pessimistic. But what's one thing you can be grateful for? Do you still have breath in your lungs? Do you have people who have stuck by your side through the suffering? Do you still have opportunities to change? When everything is going wrong, it can make us even more grateful for the things we're already grateful for!

As the adventure of the ultra comes to an end, let me encourage you: The pen is in your hand. If you're willing to allow suffering to shape your character, your life can become a pretty epic story.

ADVENTURE APPLICATION

1. When's the last time you came face to face with your limitations? What did you learn about yourself?

2. What do you usually do when suffering occurs in your life? How might you be able to shift your perspective to see the good that comes from it?

3. In which area do you need to change the most: humility, growth, or gratitude? What's one step you could take right now to get better?

ADVENTURE #2

THE TOUR DIVIDE

CHAPTER 5

A MILLION SMALL STEPS

The Tour Divide is a 2,700-mile plus bike ride from Banff, Canada to Antelope Wells, New Mexico. Riders follow the Continental Divide across the Rocky Mountains as they bike through Canada, Montana, Idaho, Wyoming, Colorado, and New Mexico before finishing up at the border of Mexico. The goal for most is to ride at around 100 miles a day. In other words, you cover the majority of North America in three to four weeks.

The race is off-road and unsupported. That means you are riding off the pavement nearly the entire time, following a route that includes four-wheeler trails, gravel roads, single track, and washed-out creek beds with boulders that make it impossible to pedal. There are many points at which the only option is to get off your bike and push, pull, or drag it.

The biggest rule of the race is that nobody is allowed to help you. However, if anything is open to the public, you're allowed to use it as well. For example, if you come across a restaurant or gas station while riding, you can eat there. The same thing goes for lodging; motels are fair game when they land along the mapped route. Participants of the Tour Divide are pretty much on their own. All you have is whatever you were able to bring with you—food, water, a change of biking clothes, and a bivy to camp out. If your bike breaks or you get injured, nobody is coming to save you.

Riders follow the route by using maps and a GPS tracker. You must stay on the route the entire time; there is a tracker who keeps an eye on all of the riders using the GPS. If you ever leave the route, you have to restart in the exact spot that you left. For example, if you need to go into town to get something, you have to hitchhike or ride back to the same place in order to start the race again. The same goes for getting off course accidentally. If you're ripping down a mountain and accidentally ride for seventeen miles on a deer trail instead of the route, you have to bike uphill seventeen more miles to where you took the wrong turn.

Maybe the best way that I can describe the Tour Divide is by using the word *unforgiving*. The mountains are unforgiving. The physical toll on your body is unforgiving. The weather and elements are unforgiving. The mistakes are unforgiving. The isolation is unforgiving. Sounds like a blast, doesn't it?!

I first discovered the Tour Divide by watching a documentary. I was browsing Netflix when I came across a movie called *Ride the Divide*. Everything about the race—from the scenery, to the difficulty, to the experiences of the riders featured in the documentary—felt like it had my name written all over it. I knew it was something that I needed to pursue. Miraculously, my family and work both gave me the okay to give a month of my life to this crazy adventure.

I flew into Banff, Canada on the day before the race. It had some of the most beautiful scenery that I'd ever seen in my life. Everywhere you looked there were breathtaking mountains, bright blue lakes, and chateau-style boutiques. There was a meal that evening for everyone who was competing in the Tour Divide the next morning. While we were eating, a guy, that everyone calls Crazy Larry, started hyping all of us up for the race. He had the riders who had never competed before raise their hands. I shot up my hand and realized I wasn't alone as the room was a mix of veterans and rookies. Out of the 198 riders who would start the journey, only sixty of them would finish. Which group would I be in? Only time would tell.

While exchanging small talk with some of the riders, I realized just how tough these guys really were. I'm not just talking about physical strength—although their muscle mass would indicate that they were physically strong—they had incredible mental strength, as well. They gave off the type of self-confidence that only comes from enduring intense elements. As butterflies suddenly began fluttering in my stomach, I couldn't help but wonder if I had what it would take.

Because I had to fly to Canada, my bike had to be reassembled that night. My friend Rick from The Cyclist Connection back home had dismantled the bike and boxed it up to be delivered. I have no clue why, but he put it in a girl's bike box to be sent to Banff. I'm sure it was quite the sight–a clueless rookie who appeared as if he was going to attempt to ride a girl's bike across North America!

At that moment, the other riders at the hostel where I was staying pretended as if they didn't notice. But we all know that it's easy to feel eyeballs on you in embarrassing situations. Which one of the riders was not like the others? That would be me! I'll never forget one guy that started talking to me. He was a sponsored rider and looked the part. The gear he had was top of the line. His outfit even matched the colors on his bike. The whole nine yards! During our conversation, it seemed like he was completely overlooking and underestimating me. His last question to me before walking away: "Do you understand how difficult this is going to be?" The truth is, I had no clue what I was in for. This would be my first overnight bike-packing experience.

Personally, I like being the underdog. I had no clue what this adventure would hold for me. So many things could go wrong with my bike, body or navigation. My plan was to give it my very best, to ride my race and to see what I was made of. For me, I knew this was a once in a lifetime opportunity. Getting ready at the starting line the next morning was pretty surreal. As I looked around and took note of all the bikes of the other riders, it became obvious that mine was on the low-end. My bike and gear had cost me about $2200—it was basically a stock bike with only a few personal modifications. From the looks of it, I'd guess that most of the other guys had spent a lot more money on theirs.

Start time had finally arrived and all of the riders began to take their places. I thought that I was at the back but quickly realized: *Oh crap, I'm at the front!* There were Tour Divide studs all around me. Josh Kato, who had won the year before, and also the legendary Mike Hall were right next to me. Mike was a veteran who could ride for days without sleep. It was unbelievable, almost like he was on autopilot! In fact, it would be this race where he would set the all-time record for the fastest completion time of the Tour Divide. It figures that's who I was toeing the start line with!

Honestly, it was all pretty intimidating for multiple reasons. For starters, I had only trained on the road. Unfortunately, where I live in Ohio just doesn't have a lot of gravel roads or single track that you can ride with a fully loaded bike where I live. It's also extremely flat. That made me feel physically underprepared. On top of that, the guys competing in this race were hardcore! They were tough, had more experience, and were riding with way better gear. I couldn't stop thinking about the question that the sponsored rider with amazing color coordination asked me: *Do you have any idea how difficult this is?*

The most accurate answer to that question was an overwhelming *no*. The truth was that I wasn't even an experienced mountain biker. Furthermore, I didn't even come close to the other riders in terms of experience. It was overly ambitious and insane to trek through the Rocky Mountains when I had never even biked off-road before!

I thought about every reason I had to be intimidated, and trust me, there were a lot of them. But while my thoughts were racing, I remembered some game-changing advice that my dad had given me as a kid playing sports: "Son, never be intimidated. It doesn't matter if your competition is bigger, faster, or stronger. You can't control them, you can only control you."

At that moment, it dawned on me that the only race I could ride was my own. That's some pretty good advice for how to approach an adventurous life. It's easy to allow intimidation to keep you living small and safe. But at the end of the day, the only person that you can control is yourself. The only race that you can ride is your own. It might look different than somebody else's, but that's okay!

I wasn't Mike Hall, Josh Kato, or a sponsored mountain biker who wore impressive outfits. My gear wasn't as good. My training and experience lacked in comparison. Those things easily could have discouraged me, but instead they ended up encouraging me. All expectations were gone. The only thing I could do every single day was wake up in the morning and continue riding my race.

ADVENTURE GUIDE TIP

For the next twenty-two days, I rode my bike an average of 117 miles per day until I finally crossed the finish line and conquered the Tour Divide. Now I have the advantage of looking at it through the rearview mirror, knowing exactly what it required of me physically and mentally. But before the race starts, you have absolutely no idea! The thought of riding a bike through the Rocky Mountains 117 miles per day for twenty-two days straight was an intimidating one. Especially when you looked around and saw the caliber of riders who would be competing in the race. It was extremely easy, and also extremely dangerous, to get too far ahead of yourself–which leads us to our Adventure Guide Tip:

ACCOMPLISHING BIG GOALS TAKES A MILLION SMALL STEPS.

I remember looking at the gigantic mountains in Banff, knowing that I'd be pedaling up them the next day, and feeling very, very small. Even worse, I knew that I'd have to do it again and again throughout Canada and five states in the US. It felt like such a monumental task that was in front of me—one that would be impossible to achieve. But do you know the only way to accomplish big goals? One small step at a time.

Maybe you're trying to get a doctorate degree, save for a house, scale your business, or become the boss at work someday. Those are all big goals that require a lot of hard work and dedication. On top of that, they definitely won't happen overnight. That's why most people never pursue their dreams or give up on them before they come true. It's easy to get overwhelmed when we feel like the place we're trying to go is over 2,700 miles away!

Trust me, I get it. The distance and difficulty of the Tour Divide was by far the greatest that I had ever been up against. The best advice that I can give you is the same advice I gave myself during the race: The only day that you have is today. Worrying about the good or bad of tomorrow won't help you. Whatever difficulties that tomorrow brings can't be defeated today, but you will destroy today by trying to do so. In the same way, it does no good to worry about what went wrong yesterday. The only moment that you have control over is the present one! **Learn from the past, prepare for tomorrow, but live fully in the moment of today.**

I believe that's one of the things that differentiated me from the other riders. Trust me, most of them outclassed me by miles, but the ability to stay present in the moment was a strength for me and a weakness for them. I was able to forget the pain of yesterday quickly. I'd often hear the guys saying things like this: "Yesterday hurt so bad. We climbed twelve thousand feet and my legs are still killing me."

The things they were holding onto so tightly, I chose not to remember. I intentionally didn't fixate on the pain of yesterday. There was nothing I could do to change it or go back and avoid it. Therefore, there was no reason to complain about it. Instead, I reflected on the beautiful scenery and small victories that I saw the day before. So much of our present reality is created by the way we think about yesterday. **Even though we might not forget the negatives of yesterday, we can choose to fixate on the positives.** That alone is enough to shift the way you approach today.

It also changes the way we face problems. We don't have to solve everything about a big problem all at once. Instead, the questions become: *What can I do today? What can I control today? Can I just make it through today?* And the next day, we can ask ourselves the same question again. It's what I call *relentless forward motion.*

I didn't finish the Tour Divide because I was bigger, faster, and stronger than the other competitors. It was because of relentless grit to keep moving forward. Regardless of what happened yesterday, or what might happen tomorrow, I just kept moving forward. Not too fast and not too slow. I rode the race as myself and went at the right pace for me.

I believe that we all have the ability to live this way. We're able to approach school, jobs, relationships, and businesses like this as well. When you stay present in the moment, it only makes sense to keep moving forward, relentlessly. The past isn't holding you back and the future isn't stopping you from moving forward.

You might be thinking: *Konan, I'm terrible at staying present in the moment. My head is either way back in the past or way ahead into the future.* The best advice that I can offer you is to try being grateful. While sitting on the saddle of my bike every day, there were moments that I literally had to remind myself to look up. Whenever I was looking down, it was easy to get caught up in my thoughts. But when I looked up and saw the beauty of nature around me, I had no option other than feeling grateful. And that gratitude led to more gratitude! I began to feel so blessed for a family who was cool with me competing in adventures and a job that allowed me to take an entire month off.

The Tour Divide was one of the most unique and beautiful experiences of my life; it would have been a shame if I didn't stay present enough to enjoy it. I wonder how many great things are unfolding in and around your life right now? Maybe you haven't taken notice because you're living too far behind in the past or too far ahead in the future. Let's choose to be people who take life a million small steps at a time. Let's breathe every adventure in and enjoy them on the way to conquering them.

ADVENTURE APPLICATION

1. Have you ever done something that you were unqualified to do? What did you learn from it?

2. Do you have difficulty staying present in the moment? If you do, what are some things you might be able to do in order to keep your mind and emotions from wandering?

3. What big goal do you currently have? Try making a plan by breaking it into small, actionable steps.

CHAPTER 6

ENDURING RAIN

The very beginning of the race was a rush of adrenaline. Just competing in such a monumental race is an exhilarating feeling, and because of that, spirits were high among all of the riders. The excitement lasted for about an hour, and then reality hit. Hard.

It was a thirty something-degree day, which is not an ideal temperature for riding a bike, especially while flying down a mountainside. The sun was completely covered by thick, dark grey clouds. And if that wasn't bad enough, it started to rain, and then kept raining. In fact, it never stopped raining for the rest of the day!

I had been cold before, but nothing even close to this extreme. During a race like this, it's not an option to go inside and warm yourself up for a few minutes. Your body has very few breaks from the elements. Weather that is cold, windy, and rainy is a nasty recipe for hypothermia.

I learned that waterproof gloves only remain waterproof for about three hours. My hands became drenched, and about eight hours into day one, I started to lose feeling. It's one thing for your fingers to go numb. Most people probably experience that at some point in their lives. Not only did my fingers go numb, but I had no feeling in my hands or lower part of my forearms. My lips turned blue as I went into the beginning stages of hypothermia.

Thank God the route led us through a park that had a small gift shop. I walked inside and saw one of the most beautiful sights possible–a hot chocolate machine. My hands were so compromised that it took me ten minutes to unzip my pack and take out my credit card. When I got to the counter, I couldn't hold my credit card to swipe it! The only option was to swallow my pride and ask the lady behind the counter for help. Thankfully, she was gracious enough to swipe my card and help me put it away.

I drank my hot chocolate while sitting on the floor of the gift shop. I was soaking wet and shaking uncontrollably. I thought: *Konan, what in the world did you just get yourself into?*

As I sat there, more riders started to come into the gift shop. The weather had beaten everybody up badly. It was almost as if the hope everyone had to start the race was leaking out all over the floor. You could see it in our faces and hear it in our voices. It reminded me of the famous Mike Tyson quote, "Everybody has a plan until they get punched in the mouth."[1] The Tour Divide had punched all of us in the mouth, and it was only day one.

It's these types of moments in life, the ones that scream for you to quit, that give you an opportunity to prove who you really are. For me, I would not get this opportunity again. I certainly didn't want to drop out of the race on day one. I picked myself up off the ground, threw my hot chocolate cup away, and got back on the saddle of my bike.

The next town was fifty miles away. Sleeping outside was not an option in my physical condition. The chilling thought of dying in my sleep crossed my mind multiple times as I pedaled. I needed to make it to civilization and find a place to stay for the night.

While riding, I came across a couple of other guys and asked them if they wanted to split a room together. Finding roommates helped you cut down costs throughout the course of the race. We agreed that whoever rode into town first would grab the room.

My hands weren't recovering as we rode, and I used the palms of my hands to change gears. However, I adapted the best that I could and gutted out those last fifty miles. I had no choice; survival mode had fully kicked into gear.

I rode into town first, grabbed us a room, and went straight to the shower. My body was craving warmth. I turned the hot water all the way up and jumped in with all of my clothes still on. It was the best shower I'd ever experienced in my entire life! I literally kept saying, "Thank you God," as I ran my hands under the water. I hung my clothes up to dry, buried myself underneath the covers, and passed out for the night.

Going to bed that night, my assumption was that I had just defeated a physical challenge that the race threw at me. *Surely,* I thought, *my body will bounce back.* There was only one problem. When I woke up the next morning, my hands were still numb. Talk about scary. To make matters worse, it was still cold and rain was in the forecast. I had no clue if my numb hands could make it through another 110-mile day in extreme weather conditions.

I laid in bed that morning and seriously debated if the right decision was to throw in the towel. Going into the race, I promised myself that I'd only quit if I was going to do permanent damage to my body. Only one day into the race, I had no clue if I had already damaged my hands forever. And if I hadn't, I wasn't sure how much more they'd be able to endure if I ever wanted them to bounce back.

I packed up my gear and started riding through the rain for a second day. Everything was now more challenging. I couldn't zip a zipper or open a bottle of water without difficulty. The question that weighed heavy on my mind was: *How much is this worth to you?* That's why some of the riders around me started to drop out of the race. They were fearful that continuing the race would cost them more than they were willing to pay.

Sleeping outside was inescapable on night two. As sunset approached, there was no civilized town anywhere close. That meant no motel room or hostel for the night. It also meant my hands would be exposed to freezing temperatures for an entire night with no hot shower or warm sheets. During the Tour Divide, most of the motels you'd come across were far from good quality. I called them *roach motels.* But after you had been on a bike all day, it didn't matter. Any room with a hot shower and warm bed felt five-star. But unfortunately, no such luxury was available that night, and I slept in the cold, drizzling rain with a group of guys in an opening in the middle of the woods.

Because the race is unsupported, the only gear you have is what you're able to carry on your back. I had brought a tent with me for situations like this, but before the race started, a veteran of the race convinced me that riding with something that heavy was not a good idea. He suggested that I purchase what's called a *bivy* from the store across the street. I had no idea what it was at the time, but walked in and asked the cashier if they had one.

She gave me the last one that the store had in stock. After I purchased it, I looked at the packaging and noticed that it said "e-bivy" on it. *Not sure what an e-bivy is,* I wondered to myself. But I packed it up without putting much more thought into it. At least until I pulled it out to use it that night.

It turns out that "e" stands for *emergency.* In other words, that type of bivy was only to be used during emergencies! A regular bivy unfolds into a structure that serves as a cocoon for you to sleep inside. It even has a zipper to completely enclose your body to protect you from the elements. My e-bivy was basically a glorified plastic bag to cover my sleeping bag—there's no zipper and very little protection! You basically pull it over your head and hope that it helps.

So, there I was in my e-bivy, in the middle of the night, laying in the cold rain. At that moment, it felt as if everything that could go wrong, did go wrong. All I had to eat was two Cliff Bars, and they both tasted disgusting! I rolled over and broke my glasses that were laying beside me. My hands still didn't have movement. It's safe to say that it wasn't my day.

I wish I could say that everything got easier on day three. It would have been great if the rain stopped and rays of sunshine broke through the clouds. To gain feeling back in my hands would have been the best feeling in the world. But none of that happened. For the next seven days, it rained for at least half of the day, every day. I rode the entire race with limited mobility in my hands. I spent more nights in that e-bivy than I'd like to remember.

Seven days in the rain was a rough way to start the race. It was not only discouraging, but it also left me and the other riders in a lot of danger. Some of you may feel like you've been living life in the rain. Maybe a dark, gloomy rain cloud has been hanging over your dreams, attitude, or emotions for what seems like forever. I get that.

But looking back, I'm thankful that I dug deep enough to make it through those seven days. Because the same thing that happened in the race also holds true for our lives. The rain always stops.

ADVENTURE GUIDE TIP

I hope to encourage those of you who feel like you're in the middle of a rainy season. Maybe nothing that you've been doing is working, you've lost the passion that used to come so naturally, or you've been in a rut and can't even remember how you got there. Regardless of the source of your rain, this next Adventure Guide Tip can help you immensely:

NEVER QUIT WHEN IT'S RAINING.

After it rained for seven days straight during the Tour Divide, I became accustomed to it. I assumed that when I woke up on day number eight it would still be raining. If we aren't careful, that's the same way that we can approach the rainy seasons of our lives. We grow accustomed to them, and sometimes even become comfortable in them. But do you know what happened on the morning of day eight of the race? I woke up and the sun was shining. And the fact that I hadn't seen the sun in such a long time made it all the more beautiful.

I promise you that the sun will shine over your dream, your adventure, or your life again. Storms never last forever. That's simply not the nature of them. And when the sun finally does shine over you again, you'll appreciate it more than you ever did before.

Whenever we are in a difficult moment, the likelihood that we will quit grows tremendously. Have you ever noticed that not many people give up on their family, job, or business when everything is going smoothly and they're hitting all of their goals? But when it starts to rain everything changes. We believe that we can only endure a storm for so long. But I wonder how many people have quit when the sun was right on the verge of coming up? During the storms of life, there is no weather report that tells us when breakthrough is going to come. Unfortunately, I've found that many people tap out just moments before the breakthrough simply because they didn't know it was on the horizon.

One of my favorite teachings comes from an acronym for the word *halt*. It's often taught to leaders of organizations or businessmen. However, it's also a good principle to live by in general. It goes like this: **Whenever we are (H)ungry, (A)ngry, (L)onely, or (T)ired, we literally should halt, or stop, before making any type of decision.** Think about it! You've probably made some of the worst decisions of your life when you were running on fumes, in a fit of rage, isolated, or exhausted.[2]

During the seven days it was raining, I knew that I wasn't in the physical, mental, or emotional state to be making big decisions about my future. Why? Because I was hungry, angry, lonely, and tired! That's right—all four! But competing in the Tour Divide was a major life goal that I wanted to accomplish. It would have been a shame if I had allowed an emotional decision to ruin a life goal right before the sun came out.

As soon as the sun came out, the entire race changed. It was still difficult. But it's amazing how a new day and a bit of sunshine can lift our spirits and give us a fresh take on life. In the same way, that dark cloud that's been hanging over your head will eventually lift. When it does, it will feel like fresh breath has been given to your lungs. You'll see everything from a completely different perspective.

That's the best place to be in when you make decisions that will likely alter your destiny.

Before we close out this chapter, let me encourage you with this: It's never as bad as you think it is. A lot of times, our own self-talk is what escalates stormy seasons and makes us believe that the rain will never end. We have to learn to ignore destructive self-chatter that goes on inside of our heads. Negative seasons stir up negative thoughts. If we can be prepared for those thoughts when we see the rain start to fall in our lives, it's much more likely that we'll be able to push through.

I promise you that the sun will come up again! Don't quit while it's raining. Your adventure depends on it.

ADVENTURE APPLICATION

1. What rainy seasons have you faced? Did you make it out on the other side?

2. What lessons have some of your toughest obstacles taught you?

3. What are some things you can do in the middle of rainy seasons to help you make it through?

CHAPTER 7

CHANGING YOUR
PERSPECTIVE

The elevation change you face while biking the Tour Divide is brutal because the path follows many forgotten paths of the Continental Divide. That means that much of your riding time is spent climbing up mountains or flying down them. Flat land was something that I would dream about! It's estimated that riders who finish the race will climb almost 200,000 feet of elevation when it's all said and done. For some perspective, that's roughly the same as summiting Mount Everest from sea-level seven times.[1]

There's a famous leg of the race called The Wall. It's name is well deserved. For starters, it feels like you're pushing your bike up a wall that's completely vertical. On top of that, many riders ironically *hit their wall* trying to make it to the top.

My best guess is that The Wall covers a 100-yard stretch of the race. There is no riding your bike to the top—only pushing. As you push, you're carrying all sorts of extra weight because of your water and gear. Your arms are straight above your head for the entire climb. Talk about a workout that sets your shoulders on fire! The footing is terrible when it's muddy. In fact, the whole time, you move two steps forward, squeeze the brake, and slide one step back. Some riders literally sit on their butts and inch backwards up the steep incline, pulling their bikes behind them.

The Wall was a crazy climb, but it definitely was not the only climb of the race. Montana was where the mountains were the steepest and the roads were the most rugged. Some of the roads were unrideable because they were washed out gulleys with huge rocks. Getting off your bike seat and pushing it uphill was a normal occurrence. On the rideable roads, some of the more experienced riders were able to sit and pedal the entire way up a mountain using their bike's highest gear. For myself, I would stand up from the saddle and pedal from that position. As a runner, that motion was more familiar and comfortable for me. Imagine getting on a training bike at the gym, setting it to the highest elevation possible, and feeling the excruciating burn in your leg muscles. Then try to picture doing that for anywhere from one to four hours! Repeat that process four times and that was an average day of riding in the Tour Divide.

After climbing a mountain for hours, I'd be dripping in sweat by the time I reached the top. That doesn't sound like a big deal, but remember, it's cold outside. Furthermore, once you go up, you must come down. As you are ripping down the other side of the mountain at twenty to thirty miles per hour, sweat-soaked clothes quickly become a problem. There were a few times that I almost went into hypothermia coming down the mountain. The longer the race went, the smarter I became. I'd take layers of clothes off right before climbing up the mountain, and put layers of clothes back on just before riding down the other side.

Another fear of riders flying down the mountain is unforeseen obstacles. A few weeks before our race, a former park ranger zipped around a corner while riding down the side of a mountain just to find a mother bear with her cubs on the trail. He hit one of the cubs, flew off his bike, and unfortunately died on the scene. During my thirty-minute rides down mountain sides, things like that would always pop into the back of my thoughts. Some guys had bells that they would ring in an attempt to scare all the wildlife away. I chose the method of singing at the top of my lungs every so often to warn the animals that I was coming. I figured that my singing voice was probably scarier than any bell I could ring!

You learn a lot of tricks like this during the Tour Divide and they often prove to be helpful along the way. However, there is no perfect ride. We already know how humbling mother nature can be from the experiences I've already shared. Sometimes she gets the best of you. I'll never forget the wipeout I had outside of Butte, Montana. Let me set the scene for you.

It was 10:30 at night and pitch-black outside. I had just finished a lot of climbing and my leg muscles were letting me know that they were unhappy about it. To make matters worse, the weather was cold, rainy, and foggy which meant even worse visibility than normal.

Despite everything working against me, I was motivated. My GPS indicated that the next town was only about twenty minutes away. I thought: *Man, if I can just make it to a hot shower and warm bed, then it will all be worth it.*

I was flying down the mountain. Fast. The thought of the comfort of a cheap hotel room probably had me more careless than I should have been. The path was wet, worn, and slippery. All of a sudden, my wheels fell into a deep rut created by a four-wheeler. I hadn't seen it in time because the light from my headlamp was dull in the rain.

The Tour Divide forces you to make a lot of split second decisions. A lot of the time, regardless of which decision you make, the result is not one that you want to experience. I didn't want to turn my handlebars to steer out of the rut because I knew that I'd flip. I opted to hit my brakes instead. Surely enough, I flipped anyway. I went flying over my handlebars and my whole world was turning upside down in slow motion.

Boom! My body hit the ground like a ton of bricks and the terrain was very unforgiving. I continued to slide further down the mountain into a puddle of fresh mud.

"Aghhhh," a subtle cry of pain slipped out. Unfortunately, nobody was around to hear me. I could only hope that nothing was broken; both on my body and bike. I laid in the mud for what seemed like an eternity in an attempt to gather my thoughts and emotions. It was a very sobering moment. The rain pounded on my face as I stared into the sky aimlessly. If I screamed, even at the top of my lungs, nobody would have been close enough to hear me. I'm not sure if I've ever felt more alone than I did at that very moment. That's when doubt started to settle deep into my soul: *Konan, what are you doing?*

Reality hit me after laying there a few minutes. I had no other choice but to get up. If I laid in that mud puddle for too long, I'd probably eventually end up dying from hypothermia. The only other option was to climb into my e-bivy for the night, which wasn't much better than laying in the mud puddle! I pushed through the pain and stood up.

Thankfully, nothing in my body was broken. However, the taillight on my bike was nowhere to be found. That became problematic as the last eight miles before town were on a main road with no street lights at 11:30 at night. Cars flew past me in the pouring rain, without having any idea I was even there. Those eight miles were full of prayers that asked God to help me survive to see the morning!

Finally, I made it into town cold, tired, and hungry as I knocked on the door of the first hotel. Of course, there was no room! I dragged myself over to the second hotel. Once again, no room. It was a horrible feeling as I was desperate to get warm and dry. Thank goodness that I finally found a hotel with one room left. I threw my bike in the room and made my way over to a convenient store, still looking like crap. I limped through the junk food aisles, exhausted, bleeding, and covered in wet mud. Right around midnight, two of my buddies from the race, Steve and Gee, entered the store. They too were looking for lodging from the rain and grabbing some food. They looked just as bad as me, which was oddly a little bit refreshing.

I'm very thankful for those guys. We had ridden together earlier and Steve had been tracking me on GPS. He was worried that something happened to me and actually called his wife. He asked her to check where my GPS dot was because he wasn't sure that I made it out of the mountains. He had even turned around to look for me.

I'm grateful for the friendships that I made on the ride. That night Steve and Gee crashed in my room. There was nothing like a hot shower and getting dry after being out in the elements all day. The next day the sun was shining and we all three headed to the bike shop for some repairs. The pain of the night before was soon behind me. However, I did learn some important lessons from the mountains.

ADVENTURE GUIDE TIP

The mountains were the most beautiful part of the Tour Divide; they were also the most painful. That's one of the greatest ironies of life: **the most worthwhile accomplishments are both beautiful and painful.**

I already mentioned that climbing up the mountains with your bike requires you to exert an unbelievable amount of effort. By the time the race was over, I had spent hours of my life fighting through excruciating pain in an attempt to make it to the top. Likewise, coming down the other side of the mountain was incredibly dangerous. The farther the ride down, the greater chance of disaster.

Even though navigating mountains was both difficult and dangerous, there was always a momentary reward that came at the top. All of the pain led to something valuable. It was on this adventure that I saw the most gorgeous views of my life. At times, I'd stop and snap a picture or film a quick video just so that I could remember the beauty at a later date. During other moments, the views were so breathtaking that I didn't want to ruin them by pulling out my phone. The best thing I could do was honor the scenery and stay present in the moment.

Not only were these views beautiful, but they taught me something valuable that leads us to an Adventure Guide Tip:

THE HIGHER THE CLIMB, THE BETTER THE VIEW.

I'm not sure if you have ever had the opportunity to take in the views from a mountaintop before. I'm grateful that the Tour Divide gave me the chance to do this many times. I noticed that the higher the mountain, the more beautiful the view. As elevation increased, so did your perspective from the top of the mountain. The highest mountains provided the hardest journeys to the top, but also the most stunning pictures.

The higher a mountain is, the fewer people have seen the top. Why? Great views take a great amount of work. The same holds true in your life. To have anything great, you must exert a great amount of effort. A great marriage takes work. A great relationship with your kids takes work. A great grade on your presentation takes work. A great business takes work. The truth is, nobody is going to hand you anything worthwhile. The things that we've actually worked for are always more rewarding.

Looking back, it would have been easy to allow the pain of climbing each mountain to blind my eyes from the beauty at the top. Pain can lead to tunnel vision. We can sometimes want painful moments to end so badly that we solely focus on finishing the race so that whatever is causing the pain will quit bothering us. As a driven person, I definitely understand that type of philosophy. However, it can also get us into trouble.

When we fail to recognize the beauty in the pain, we miss the good and become consumed with the bad. It's how tough seasons of friendship eventually just become tough friendships. It's why difficult seasons in business turn into discouragement, doubt, and eventually the death of a dream. One thing that I've learned in life is the importance of the pause.

During the Tour Divide, I did my best to pause periodically and take in the views from on top of the mountains. At times, I would even take ten or fifteen minutes to eat my lunch up there and appreciate the beauty. It's one of the things that helped me to keep going. In the middle of a painful experience, beautiful things were also unfolding.

Think about your life for a second. What is currently causing you pain?

- Can family be frustrating? Absolutely! But the bond that is formed in some of the most difficult moments is also beautiful.
- Is your business experiencing some loss? Loss never feels good, but it does teach us some important lessons to help us grow even more in the future.
- Has your dream been unfolding slower than you assumed that it would? I know—delay is one of the most difficult things to process. But it also develops your patience, which helps build your character and relationships.

I don't know your pain, but I do know that on the other side of it, your view of life will be even better than it is right now. So keep climbing!

ADVENTURE APPLICATION

1. What's the most beautiful sight that you've ever seen? What did it cost you to make the journey to see it?

2. Think of some things in your life right now that you perceive as negatives. Write down some positives that are coming from, or will come from, what feels difficult right now.

CHAPTER 8

MAKING MEMORIES

The beginning of the Tour Divide was defined by difficulty. I'm talking brutal weather, washed-out mountain trails, and extreme physical adjustments that your body has to make. But in every adventure or new experience, there comes a point when you start to get the hang of things. It was during the last half of the race that I figured out how to ride, sleep, and eat well.

I developed more and more of a rhythm each day, and even started to move through legs of the race more quickly than anticipated. On the backend, I got stronger and my daily mileage continued to increase. Throughout the race, I'd find myself catching up to one group of guys, riding with them for a while, and then moving on to a group that was farther ahead. I'd push myself to catch up with the next group, and when I finally got to them, their momentum would pull me along.

My original goal was to reach the border of Mexico and finish the race in twenty-five days. As my pace increased, I realized that I was going to beat that goal. I decided to set a new one to keep myself motivated. If everything went according to my new plan, it was realistic for me to get home by the Fourth of July. The thought of seeing my kids again was the fuel I needed to keep moving forward with everything inside of me. For the first time, conquering the Tour Divide was actually within my reach.

I was riding through New Mexico at night about 160 miles away from the end of the race. My goal was to make it another forty to sixty miles before bed so that I could cross the finish line the next day. If everything went according to plan, I'd be home by the Fourth to see my family. Everything was going smoothly until my bike tires hit the Continental Divide Trail.

The CDT was a hiking trail that only lasted for a small trek of the race—a few miles at the most. Physically, it wasn't an overly challenging trail to cross. In my mind, I thought I'd breeze through it on my way to finishing up the mileage for the night. But my assumption and reality ended up being polar opposites.

The trail was razor thin and extremely technical. There were many turns and rocks that you had to navigate around on your fully loaded bike. It was nothing new, and I had gotten used to this type of riding throughout the race. However, there were a few major problems. First of all, it was once again completely dark outside and my lights weren't providing enough light for me to clearly see all of the twists, turns, and obstacles that were in my path. Secondly, the trail was along a steep mountainside. One small mistake and not only would I fail to finish the race, but I'd probably plummet to my death.

My tires slipped near the edge of the trail a few times and that was enough to convince me to stop! I pushed my bike ten feet off the side of the trail, pulled that darn e-bivy out of my backpack, and set up camp for the night. Before sliding underneath my plastic sheet, I opened up a huge danish in the hope of eating my emotions. By that point, I missed my family very badly. My hope of spending a holiday with them had grown a lot before this delay. The reality of 160 miles being too much to ride the next day now weighed on my mind. It was a really down moment for me. I remember dozing off to sleep feeling very discouraged.

However, I woke up before the sun even came up and felt like a new man. It's amazing how each new day brings new possibilities and fresh perspectives. As daylight struck, I could see much better, and navigated the technicality of the narrow trail with much greater ease. After conquering that leg of the race, my pace picked up and I started to make great time once again. It was then that a crazy thought popped into my head: *Maybe I could do all 160 miles and finish...today.*

When you've been on a journey as long as the Tour Divide, when the end finally comes into sight, all bets are off. Thinking of the finish line was plenty of fuel to my fire. It was pedal to the metal from here on out!

In order to finish, I'd have to ride many miles farther than I had on any other single day of the race. I was a little bit nervous about destroying my body or injuring myself before crossing the finish line. But at the same time, I was determined to gut it out and complete the race. I pushed, and pushed, and pushed some more.

The last sixty miles of the race was pavement. During an off-road race, it's an absolute relief when your tires hit the pavement. Only about eight percent of the 2,700 miles are on pavement. As a skinny guy who isn't necessarily built for climbing up mountains on muddy trails, riding on a smooth surface energized me mentally and emotionally.

My back tire was slowly leaking, which meant every hour I had to stop and pump it up. But at that point, it didn't matter. Excitement started to rise up inside of me as reality hit: I was actually going to conquer the Tour Divide.

The last leg of the race was in the middle of nowhere. It was one-road-in and one-road-out to the Mexican border. Every so often a car would pass as I rode along, but I'd never look up or pay much attention to the drivers. I was too focused. All of a sudden, I felt the presence of a car slowing down and riding right next to me. I looked up and saw my dad, smiling from ear-to-ear and rolling down his window.

"Son!" he shouted as we rode next to each other.

"Hey Pop!" I responded. I'd never been more thankful to see my dad before. It actually brought tears to my eyes.

"I can't believe it, son, you did it! We're so proud of you. We've been following your dot on the GPS every night. Your mother can't go to sleep until she sees where you're sleeping for the night. 'My baby is stuck in the mountains,' she'd say. But now you're finishing!"

We probably talked for a good half-hour as he rode beside me. Finally, he drove ahead to wait for me at the finish line. Another rider caught up to me and we rode the last few miles together. I'll never forget seeing the finish line in the distance. We crossed it together as my dad was standing there cheering for us. I laid my bike down and Dad gave me a giant bear hug. It was one of the most surreal feelings that I've ever experienced.

I conquered the Tour Divide in twenty-two days, averaging 117-miles per day. Not too bad for a rookie! Out of the 198 riders who started, I was one of the 60 to finish. For most of the riders, crossing the finish line is one of the biggest accomplishments of their lives. It was the same for me. But do you know what's crazy?

There were no medals or trophies. There wasn't a crowd waiting at the finish line to recognize my achievement. It was really just me, my dad, and the unspoken understanding that I had just accomplished something incredible. At the end of the day, it was even more special to me to share the experience of a lifetime with my lifelong hero–my dad–than be rewarded with any kind of trophy.

There's a sign at the finish line for the U.S. Customs and Border Protection that divides the United States from Mexico. It's where all the riders who finish the Tour Divide take their picture. I lifted my bike above my head, which felt like an impossible feat considering how weak I was, and my dad snapped my victory photo. We got to our hotel and I took my shirt off. Not only did I smell bad from four days with no shower, but I was so skinny that you could see the ribs on my back. But as I looked at myself in the mirror, smelly, skinny, and all, I knew I'd just accomplished something that would change me forever.

ADVENTURE GUIDE TIP

The Tour Divide is one of those experiences that is grueling in the moment, but when you reflect on the experience, you'd give anything to go back. It was an adventure that was filled with the most beautiful sights I've ever seen. It introduced me to an entire new way of living; a life outside of the daily luxuries that we take for granted. It literally forced me to climb to heights that I'd never before achieved. But looking back on it all, it wasn't the scenery, sleeping in the wild, or climbing to the top of a mountain that I'll remember the most. It was having the privilege of sharing a special moment at the finish line with my dad. It leads me to my last Adventure Guide Tip that I learned during the Tour Divide:

MAKE MEMORIES WITH THE PEOPLE WHO MATTER THE MOST.

Too often in life, we move on too quickly from one adventure to the next without ever stopping to celebrate. In our drive, we can easily fall into the trap of only thinking about what's next. I've learned the importance of not just living in the moment, but also enjoying the moment. Riding next to my dad and giving him a smelly bear hug at the finish line is a moment that I genuinely enjoyed. I'll cherish it for the rest of my life.

I've been encouraging you throughout this book to go live your adventure by choosing experiences that will shape you. We don't have to be yanked through life while holding on for dear life! We have the ability to take control through intentionality. That's why I'm the crazy guy who competes in a new limit-testing adventure every year. Those are the experiences that I want to have. They shape me into the person that I want to become.

And while experiences mold us into who we are, sharing that moment at the Tour Divide with my dad taught me that people are even more important. Here's another way to think about it: **life isn't just about what you do, it's about who you do it with.**

The quality of your life is the sum of your experiences and relationships. Experiences that you're passionate about—biking through the mountains, serving impoverished communities overseas, starting your dream non-profit—all add value to your life. In the same way, people who you really care about, and who really care about you, add so much joy to your life. When you can combine experiences that you love with people that you love, you create a life that's worth living. That's the very definition of a memory.

At the end of our lives, one of the only things that we'll have left is our memories. The size of our house, cost of our cars, or title at work won't matter anymore. But the memories that we made with loved ones will mean everything. And I think we can be intentional about creating some of those.

You might be asking: *How do I go about creating memories that matter?* My answer: **invest into what you love with who you love.** That moment with my dad took investment. Not only from myself, but also from my dad. I invested in a bike, a plane ticket, money for food and hotels, training, and even sacrificed a month of my life. My dad made an investment in our relationship when he flew across the country just to be there for me at the finish line. My investment was in what I loved, and his in who he loved. Together, we created a memory that will last forever.

The most important questions you can answer are: *Who do I love? What do I love? How can I invest in those things?* For some of you, that might look like saving enough money to take your family on vacation. For others, it might be going on a mission trip with friends from your church. Maybe you even need to make an investment into becoming a better leader so you can help friends succeed at their dreams. It will look different for all of us, but we all have the opportunity to make memories.

One of my favorite movie series is *The Lord of the Rings*. It follows the story of a hobbit named Frodo who was chosen to destroy a ring that could bring evil and destruction to many if left in the wrong hands. He takes his friend, Sam, on the journey with him, and also meets up with two well-meaning troublemaker hobbits named Merry and Pippin. On their journey to Mount Doom, where the ring must be destroyed, they encounter an unbelievable amount of obstacles and challenges. Still, against all odds, they destroy the ring, save the world, and return to their home—the Shire.[1]   During one of the last scenes, the four friends are sitting at a pub together after their incredible adventure. Everyone around them was dancing, laughing, and having a good time. Meanwhile, Frodo, Sam, Merry, and Pippin share a pint and just look at each other. They didn't have to talk about their experience; they lived it. Nobody else knew, and nobody else had to know. The friends knew. And they also knew they'd never be the same.

I don't know about you, but those are the types of memories I want to share with the most valuable people in my life. Ones that mean something to us, even if they don't mean anything to anybody else. The types of memories that will change us forever. Those are the types of memories that we all have the opportunity to create. Let's be memory-makers!

ADVENTURE APPLICATION

1. Who are some of the most important people in your life? Do you invest in those relationships on a regular basis?

2. What are some of your best memories? What made them valuable to you?

3. What are some events on your bucket list? Who would you like to experience those events with? Start making a plan to actually put action toward making those memories!

ADVENTURE #3

GRAND CANYON RIM TO RIM TO RIM

CHAPTER 9

OBSERVATION VS. ACTION

Onto the next adventure! Completing the Grand Canyon Rim to Rim to Rim Challenge is a badge of honor in the ultra-marathon community. The task is pretty straight-forward. Start at one rim of the Grand Canyon, run down the side wall, run across the floor and up the opposite side wall, or rim, then run back to the rim where you started. In other words, anyone crazy enough to take on the challenge runs from rim to rim, and then back to the rim where they started. When it's all said and done, runners go down a side wall twice, up a side wall twice, and across the floor of the Grand Canyon twice.

If you've never been to the Grand Canyon, it truly is an experience to behold. I will never forget seeing it for the first time with my own eyes. It literally took my breath away. The Grand Canyon is 277 miles long, eighteen miles wide, and one mile deep.[1] In fact, because of its length, it takes over four hours just to drive from one rim of the canyon to another. There are a few trails that runners follow when they're attempting to go rim to rim to rim. The path that I chose ended up being a total distance of forty-four miles roundtrip.

Attempting the challenge is highly discouraged by park rangers because of the danger that comes with it. At the starting location there's actually a sign that reads: Do not attempt to go to the bottom and back to the top in the same day. Underneath is a picture of a man who is completely red, hunched over, and throwing up. Very encouraging! Ironically enough, I ended up looking like that man by the end of the race.

There are multiple factors that make the challenge dangerous. For starters, the heat is extreme, especially at the bottom of the canyon. Runners are strongly discouraged from attempting the feat in the summer because it is just too hot. Your body would shut down from heat exhaustion. There's also the issue of water. The day before I started, I went to the park rangers and asked if the water pipes inside of the canyon were working. If they weren't, it would have been a no-go. Without water, dehydration would be inevitable as it's just too far and hot. And to top it all off, there's no cell phone service! If something goes wrong, you are all on your own to figure it out.

The day before the run, I checked out the views from the top of the Grand Canyon. My photographer friend Ricky made the trip with me to help capture the moment. At that moment, I understood why it was the second most visited national park in the United States. Looking across the vast array of chiseled red rock was stunning. Undoubtedly, that's where mother nature chose to do some of her most beautiful work.

That's when the enormity of the challenge hit me in the face. It's one thing to dream, plan, and train for something. It's a whole other thing when you are there and start to wonder what in the world you were thinking? The next day, there would be no turning back. In just a few hours, I would test my metal against the Grand Canyon. I was definitely excited, but it also seemed like a monumental task.

For this adventure, you want to get started as early as possible. A forty-four-mile run, with nearly thirty of the miles being up or down a canyon wall, eats up a majority of the day. Starting early gives you more time to navigate complications just in case you come along some. On top of that, the more of the race you can knock out before the blistering hot sun is at its peak, the better.

My adventure officially started at 4:00 a.m. It was still cold outside, probably in the low forties. I had a light jacket on; I ended up ditching it as soon as the sun came out. It was still dark outside, which meant relying on my trusted headlamp as I ran down the South Kaibab Trail for roughly seven miles. The descent was very rugged with huge steps and loose rocks the entire way down.

Being inside of the Grand Canyon at night is a unique experience. I couldn't see very far in front of me because the brightness from my headlamp was swallowed by the darkness of the early morning. Even though I couldn't see it, I could feel that I was in the middle of a vast expanse. I was all alone in complete silence, but even still, there was no echo of noise. There are no rails to keep you safe as you run down the side wall. If you took a misstep, you were looking at a 300-plus foot drop. It felt like I was literally running into the depths of the unknown.

Coming down into the canyon, I hit a spot where I couldn't locate the trail in the dark. I ended up looking around for forty minutes without any luck. The only option that I had was to sit down and wait for thirty more minutes for the sun to come up. I was pretty ticked. I didn't know exactly how difficult the journey ahead of me would be, but I did know that every single minute was valuable. Finally the sun came up and I was on my way again.

As soon as I found the trail, two other runners who were attempting the challenge caught me. It turned out there were five of us attempting the challenge that day—two men from New Zealand and two women from Florida. I ran with the two New Zealanders for a little while before they went on ahead of me. They were some *tough* guys. They flew all the way across the globe just to compete in this challenge. That type of extreme adventure is what they dedicated their lives to do.

The sun started to clearly illuminate the bottom of the canyon and it was *breathtaking*. This was by far the best part of the challenge. I ran across a bridge that takes you over the Colorado River. The canyon was nice and flat, plus the footing was pretty good. The way that the scenery hits you after running in the dark for so long was unforgettable. You were up close and personal with beautiful creeks, cacti that grow colorful flowers, and beautiful red rocks everywhere that you look.

As I ran, I fully understood that this adventure would get much tougher the longer the day went on. The sun would get hotter, the miles would feel longer, and my body would feel weaker. But the first leg of the race was very enjoyable. It didn't come without challenges, but the surrealness of being inside the Grand Canyon is something that's hard to explain to someone who never has been. The vast beauty of mother nature is something that I will never forget.

ADVENTURE GUIDE TIP

I'm one of the few people on the planet who has had the unique experience of seeing the Grand Canyon from the top and bottom. You might not guess it, but the different perspectives really are completely different from one another. Looking across the canyon from across the rim is beautiful; however, you're also examining everything from afar. But looking across the canyon from inside of the canyon itself is quite a different story! Everything is up close and personal. You don't have to guess what the texture of the rock is like, you can literally reach out and feel it. The streams no longer just look refreshing from a distance. You can reach down, scoop two handfuls of water, and wash your face off.

Being in the Grand Canyon makes you feel like you're a little fish in a huge pond. It makes sense, as it is a whopping 1,904 square-miles, after all. For most of your time down there, you don't see anybody else but yourself. You're all alone in a vast land of beauty. At that moment, nothing else going on anywhere in the world seems important anymore. It almost feels as if you are one with one of the seven natural wonders of the world.

The people who remain at the top don't get that type of experience. Sure, they enjoy it from a distance, but nothing beats being up close and personal. It actually reminds me a lot of the way we experience life. Those who dive in tend to live more fully than those who simply observe from a distance. That principle leads us to our Adventure Guide Tip:

LIVING FROM THE INSIDE-OUT IS BETTER THAN LOOKING FROM THE OUTSIDE-IN.

Truthfully, a lot of people resonate with standing on the outside of their lives and looking in. What do I mean by that? There are areas in all of our lives that we simply don't engage in. **It's always easier to observe than to take action. But those who live a life of observation also live a life of regret.**

Here's a crazy statistic: Out of the five-million tourists that visit the Grand Canyon each year, less than one percent of them ever descend below the rim.[2] Watching is easy; action is work! It would have required a lot less effort to take in the view from above, snap a few pictures, and fly home. But less effort also leads to lesser reward. Even still, there are a lot of obstacles that keep us in *observation mode* and out of *action mode*. Let me share some of the biggest with you:

1. Fear

Fear tries to protect us from unknowns by telling us that it's safer to just sit on the sidelines and stay away from danger. While fear is genuinely concerned about us, it doesn't understand that a life of timidity and passivity is dangerous in its own way. The things that we miss out on can hurt us even more than the things we're attempting to stay safe from. If we want to live our adventures, it requires that we stick our neck out there sometimes. We must apply for the job we don't feel qualified to do, take the opportunity that's out of our comfort zone, and try new things even when we're unprepared!

2. Lack of Time

Sometimes we don't take action because we don't have time for the things we're passionate about. Busyness is one of the sneakiest threats to living a life full of adventure. You can get so caught up in going to work, paying the bills, soccer practices, and staying afloat that your life can pass by you in the blink of an eye. Before you know it, you haven't intentionally worked on your health, marriage, or dreams. We must create space and margins in our lives to take action steps toward the things that matter most to us.

3. Insecurity

Insecurity will keep you from living a full life. It always asks the questions: *Do you really think you deserve this? What makes you think that you, of all people, can chase after your dreams?* I've learned that **who we are always precedes what we do.** For example, if you refuse to accept that you're intelligent, you probably won't apply to a prestigious school. If you believe that you're not athletic, you'll never try out for the team. And if you allow your past to define you, you'll settle for a future that's less than what you deserve. Action-oriented people are usually those who have overcome their insecurities.

4. Fatigue

Regardless of what we like to believe, everybody requires rest and boundaries to operate at their best. I believe that most people are gifted enough to accomplish their goals. Talent isn't typically the issue. Many people struggle to structure their lives in such a way that they have enough energy for the things that matter most. A well-rested person who is less talented will always accomplish more than an exhausted person who is extraordinarily gifted. Fatigue will keep us away from the action simply because we're too tired to engage. The famous saying is true: "Fatigue makes cowards of us all."

5. Apathy

Apathy happens when we become disinterested in what used to make our hearts come alive. Discouragement and disappointment can all lead to living apathetically. If a sense of adventure is going to overcome our apathy, we must choose to let go of our pain from the past in order to reclaim our passion. Whatever hurt you doesn't have to define you! Unless you choose to stay in observation mode because of it.

Here is a bit of advice for the end of this chapter: Get back in the game! I grew up as a basketball player and I know the difference between standing on the sidelines and being a part of the action. The sidelines are where you come to rest and recharge. However, no competitor wants to stay there for too long. The game is where you're able to have the most impact and influence.

In the same way, if you want your life to have impact and influence, you have to choose to play. Engage the action. Confront the challenges. Overcome the obstacles. At the end of your life, you'll either remember the observations you made or the action you took. Let's be people who live from the inside-out instead of looking from the outside-in!

ADVENTURE APPLICATION

1. Are you naturally more likely to observe or take action when it comes to something you're passionate about? Why do you think

that is?

2. Which of the five observation mode obstacles do you struggle with the most: fear, lack of time, insecurity, fatigue, or apathy? What might help you to overcome it?

CHAPTER 10

OVERCOMING EMOTIONS

The start of the Rim to Rim to Rim Challenge came with difficulties, but overall was pretty enjoyable. The canyon floor was completely covered in shade the first time I ran across it. It created the perfect temperature to take in the perfect scenery. However, what started as enjoyable quickly turned into exhausting.

It all started when I stopped at a water station to fill up before starting my first ascent up the opposite wall. I had already made it down the first outer wall and all the way across the floor of the canyon. Making it to the top of this outer wall would require a seven-mile climb up the North Kaibab Trail. The top would officially mark the halfway point of the adventure, which was twenty-two miles. However, things started to get sketchy when I stopped to fill up my water bottle before making the grueling climb.

The day before, the park ranger had assured me that all of the pipes were in working condition. But the closer I got to the water station, the sound of a loud *hiss* echoed through the canyon. I looked up, and sure enough, water was shooting out of a busted pipe. *Crappp!*

Not sure when, or if, I'd have access to water again, I drank as much as my body would allow. Your stomach is the most important water bottle that you have. I also filled up my two-liter CamelBak and two smaller bottles that I carried to stay hydrated. I added my Go Far hydration mix to all of my bottles, which provides calories that your body needs just from your drink. Then I pressed on and hoped for the best.

The climb up the North Kaibab Trail was absolutely brutal. Running seven miles up a wall of the Grand Canyon is a high-intensity workout. Conquering the climb drained me more than I would have liked to admit. And there's no comfort when you reach the top of the canyon, either. It was like a ghost town, with not another soul in sight, due to being closed for the season. There was a bathroom but no water. I found a tall tree, laid down in the dirt, and stared up at the sky.

It was at that moment that I knew I was in trouble. I decided to give myself fifteen minutes to refuel and regain composure. My body laid on the ground like deadweight, completely exhausted. But even though my body was at rest, my mind continued to run at full speed. Thoughts of fear creeped into my brain and started to take over: *Konan, you know yourself very well from all these years of pushing your body to its limits. Right now, you've burned through three-fourths of your energy. That means you only have a quarter-tank left, at the most. The problem is that you still have half of this challenge to go! It's not possible; you don't have what it takes.*

I spent those fifteen minutes in an intense mental battle. After weighing all options, the conclusion I came to was that there was no other option but to press on. Seriously, what else could I do? There was no cell service, which meant I couldn't call my photographer, Ricky, who was waiting for me on the other side of the canyon for help. And even if he could read my mind, it would be a four-hour drive for him to come and pick me up. The only way back to safety was via the same way in which I had come—a twenty-two mile run through the Grand Canyon. Except now I'd be running on fumes.

I stood up, stretched, and geared up to take off running once again. I intentionally shifted the narrative of my thoughts away from the fear that had started to consume me to thoughts that were determined to finish no matter what. There's no room for toxic thoughts during a challenge of that magnitude; they can literally kill you if you're not careful.

I knew that it wouldn't be easy. Furthermore, I knew it was going to be an incredibly long day. The reality that I'd have to push myself further than perhaps I ever had in a single day before settled on me. It was time to suck it up, buttercup. The Grand Canyon picked a fight with me, and it was time to punch back. Sometimes it takes our backs being up against the wall to really prove what we're capable of. My back was definitely against the wall, and I was about to find out how much grit I had inside.

I took a deep breath and started to head down the North Kaibab

Trail. The one thing that I didn't think about before the challenge started was how difficult running down the canyon walls would be. In my head, climbing up would be the only part that really proved to be challenging. But on the way down, you really can't stop much and even feel out of control during steep stretches with loose footing. By the end of it, my quads were completely spent.

I reached the bottom and the canyon started to heat up like an oven as the sun settled directly overhead. All of my training was during springtime in Ohio; where it was anywhere between forty and fifty degrees. But the springtime in Colorado—specifically, at the bottom of the Grand Canyon—was close to 100 degrees. It was double the temperature that my body had gotten used to and, trust me, I was feeling it.

The ground was hot, the canyon walls were hot, and my skin was baking. My face was on fire and I began to not feel so well. It was at that moment, with about fifteen miles left to go, I realized I was likely experiencing the first signs of heat exhaustion.

The toxic thoughts—along with some negative emotions—that I thought I left at the top rim returned. I had legitimate questions about how much more I could endure. But once again, I had to choose how I would respond to those thoughts. Would I control them, or would I allow them to control me? I took a swig of water, careful to conserve as much as I could for the next leg of the challenge. I forced myself to think positively: *Konan, you're going to make it.*

I picked up one leg, then another, and kept moving forward relentlessly.

ADVENTURE GUIDE TIP

Whenever someone says *strength*, we naturally think of physical strength. Especially within the context of living our adventure. It's true that physical strength is extremely important. However, from my experience, I've found that mental strength is equally important.

In many cases, it might be even more important!

During the Rim to Rim to Rim Challenge, my body was capable of more than it was giving off. I was experiencing heat exhaustion and dehydration. Because of that, my body was screaming at me to throw in the towel. And at first, I was convinced that its concerns were valid. However, when I became intentional about my thoughts, they were able to remind my body that we could push farther and achieve more. This leads us to our Adventure Guide Tip:

YOUR BODY ACHIEVES WHAT YOUR MIND BELIEVES.

So much of our lives comes down to who we will allow to rule us. The body and the mind are constantly fighting for control of our actions. The question we all must answer is this: Will my body rule my mind, or will my mind rule my body?

Whenever we allow our bodies to lead based on feelings or emotions, we end up in trouble 99 percent of the time. Emotions aren't leaders, they're followers. What does that mean? Another way to say it is that they are *reactionary*. They are signals that your body gives you based on the pleasure or pain that you're experiencing.

I'm not saying that emotions are all bad. A lot of the time they give us valuable insight as to what is going on inside of us. They just don't make good leaders. If we allowed our emotions to rule us, we'd likely become lazy and lethargic people who struggle to get out of bed. Think about it! If we were to give into every appetite of craving that we *feel* like we want, we'd all end up making some serious messes in our lives.

This might sound pretty intense, but stay with me for a second. You must force your body to become your slave. The goal is to get our bodies to work for us instead of us working for our bodies. The body is a great tool when it's a slave. It has the ability to play sports, run marathons, build things, climb mountains, and endure obstacles. Competition, passion, creation, and extreme joy can all come from what the human body has the ability to do. But only when the body is our slave and not our master.

You might be asking: *What do I do if my emotions and feelings have taken the lead?* That's a great question. It's not as simple as suppressing them. After all, emotions are great indicators of what's going on deep inside of us. For example, when heat exhaustion hit me, my body felt that it was in danger. It communicated that through the emotion of fear. It's good to be aware when your body has concerns. But it's also important to realize that emotions tend to be a little dramatic.

Emotions don't share their concerns calmly or rationally. They don't provide you with a well-thought out explanation that helps weigh the pros and cons during intense situations. Nope! They always scream at you. They're often loud, irrational, and outspoken. Because of their nature, we can't just ignore emotions. And that's not a smart thing to do! **We can't choose whether or not we hear our emotions, but we can choose whether or not we will listen to them.**

Hearing and listening are very different. Hearing is inevitable, but listening is intentional. When my emotions were screaming for me to quit during the challenge, I intentionally chose not to listen. When I thought about it rationally, they didn't make much sense anyways. I couldn't quit in the middle of the Grand Canyon with no cell phone service and no way out. Taking a seat on the floor of the canyon surely would have killed me. The only thing that made actual sense was to push through and keep moving.

It's our responsibility to bring rationality to the irrationality of our emotions. The characteristics of our emotions are what make them the spice of life. But those same characteristics will take us farther than we want to go and keep us longer than we want to stay.

For example, it's emotion that fills our hearts with love and deep passion for another person. But those same emotions can make you intensely angry and frustrated over small issues in the relationship. They'll not only make a small problem a big problem, but they'll hold a grudge over that problem for way longer than what's necessary. In the same way, the nerves you get before giving a speech or presentation are healthy. They remind you that it's important to prepare. But if that fear paralyzes you and keeps you from delivering the message, you might fail your class or lose your job.

Emotions are weapons. But our minds help us determine whether those weapons work for us or against us. They either help us to crush our goals, or they turn around and crush us.

As this chapter comes to an end, maybe the best first step you can take to control your emotions is to develop a plan. When all of my kids were about to start middle school, I had a talk with each of them about peer pressure. I warned them that they'd inevitably be offered drugs, alcohol, and other things that are destructive to their future. And right there, before the peer pressure actually happened, we came up with a plan of what they were going to do when it did. In the same way, we must become aware that our emotions will scream in moments of weakness and try to steer us off course. We have the ability to develop a response plan now, so that we can keep moving forward in our lives of adventure!

ADVENTURE APPLICATION

1. Which of the following emotions are the most common for you: excitement, fear, passion, anger, happiness, or anxiousness? What do you think is the source of your strongest emotions?

2. Does your mind control your body or does your body control your mind? How do you think you could develop more mental strength?

3. What are you going to do the next time that negative emotions try to take you farther than you want to go and keep you longer than you want to stay?

CHAPTER 11

DEEP PLACES

Phantom Ranch is a campground that's inside of the Grand Canyon itself. It's such a unique experience to stay there that you have to book a room a year in advance. It's located right across the river from the south wall. This is right before the place where I would begin my final seven-mile ascent up the Bright Angel Trail. It was a different wall than I had descended down to start the race at four in the morning. Now, late afternoon was about to hit, and I saw Phantom Ranch in the distance.

During the tough moments of running across the blistering canyon floor, I dreamed of the moment I'd see Phantom Ranch. It meant I'd get to catch my breath inside of a glorious air-conditioned building. It also meant a quick break for my weary legs. But maybe what I was most excited about was a bag of salty potato chips and an ice-cold Coke.

I walked into the snack shack; I'm sure that I was looking and smelling like garbage. Unfortunately, there weren't any potato chips or Coke on the menu, so I settled for a lemonade and a bag of pretzels. Even still, just to sit down at a table in the miniature snack area was incredible. As a bonus, the lady sitting at a table next to me was kind and struck up a conversation. It was a much needed distraction from how beat up my body was feeling.

"So, what are you doing out here today?" she asked. I'm sure she could see and smell that I was doing something out of the ordinary.

"I'm running from rim to rim to rim," I started to explain. "But uh—you'll have to excuse me."

"Sir, are you okay?" she asked with a concerned look on her face.

I suddenly had that horrible feeling you get right before you throw up. The lemonade wasn't sitting well with me. It felt like it had violently turned on me, creating knots in my stomach. It took a quick sprint for me to make it outside the front door of the snack shack and around the corner of the storefront. There, I sat down and repeatedly spilled my cookies all over the floor of the Grand Canyon.

Crappp, I thought to myself. I tried to keep my composure

but inwardly began to panic ever so slightly. One of the dangers of dehydration is that you can become too far gone. If that happens, the only way to bounce back is to get an IV at the hospital. I knew from experience because I have seen it happen to other athletes. I desperately wanted to avoid it happening to me!

I continued to sip on the lemonade and eventually transitioned to water, but my stomach was not cooperating. My body needed liquid but my stomach wouldn't hold it down. My muscles started to cramp and lose function.

I sat there, not only feeling defeated and discouraged but also in a state of danger. Then I decided I could sit there no longer. The longer I remained stagnant the more I wanted to stay there. There were seven miles left, and I knew that they were going to require absolutely every ounce of grit that I had inside of me.

I filled up my water bottles for the journey ahead. As I was preparing to take off again, some of the people who had witnessed my vomiting came over to check on me.

"Are you going to be able to make it?" they asked, concerned.

"Yeah," I replied, not totally sure myself. "But I have to get going."

And just like that, I got back on the trail and started walking. Slowly but surely, I began to feel slightly better. Pretty soon, my walk turned into a jog and my pace became steady. I started making pretty good time again. And then, *boom*! It hit me once more and I hunched over and threw up again. Looking back, lemonade probably wasn't the best idea!

There were about four miles left to go, and I could feel the energy leaving my body. Each time that I vomited, I became a little bit more depleted. I found a rock to rest on for a while, knowing that I was in pretty rough shape. The salt from sweating all day in such a dry place was now crusted on the side of my face. I was looking rough.

I got up and began making my way once again up the canyon wall, battling against my stomach and my brain the entire time.

That's when I heard a voice that almost seemed to be yelling at me. I was a little bit disoriented, and thought that I might be hallucinating or hearing things like I did during the ultramarathon! But when I looked up, there was a highly concerned middle-aged lady all up in my face and personal space.

"Sir!" she exclaimed. "OH MY GOSH—you look terrible!"

I acknowledged her with a half-hearted wave and head nod. Whenever I get to this type of depleted physical state, it becomes difficult to talk. My voice only projects at the volume of a whisper. It would have been easier to remain silent, but my newly found friend wasn't giving up that easily.

"Sir, what are you trying to accomplish out here?"

"I started here, I went over there, and now I'm coming back here," I whispered back, knowing that I probably wasn't making much sense.

"That's crazy! Do you realize that people die out here?"

I nodded.

"You think you're going to make it another four miles? Sir, you're going to be one of those people. You are going to die out here. My son and I have an extra tent. Camp out with us and you can finish your crazy challenge in the morning!

The morning, I thought. *You don't understand, my plane leaves in the morning.* Somehow, even in my delirious state, I was able to remember the details of my flight itinerary.

I responded with the most clarity I could muster in that moment, but even still, slurring my words: "My friend is at the upper rim waiting for me. I'm going to go a little further, and if I can't make it, I'll turn around and find you."

She wasn't happy and began to raise her voice at me, "Be reasonable sir, be reasonable!" Truthfully, I didn't know if she was going to try to restrain me. I didn't have the energy to put up a fight if she did. She could have tackled me right there and knocked me to the ground with ease. I was no better than deadweight at that moment.

I jogged ahead in seemingly slow motion. Only a quarter-mile from my confrontation with the crazy lady, I threw up again. I sat on a log while my body worked hard to discard everything that it had inside of it. I thought to myself: *Dude, what are you doing? Are you actually going to die out here?* It was a scary moment.

I finally hit the three-miles-to-go mark and told myself that it would be just like running a 5K. That's something I had accomplished hundreds of times. Obviously this was different, but the shift in perspective lifted my spirits.

Toward the end of the challenge, the sun started to set. I had told my photographer, Ricky, who was also my ride, that my goal was to be done in fifteen hours. I also told him that if I wasn't finished by the seventeen-hour mark, something was wrong. It was now encroaching on seventeen hours. And I suppose that something was also borderline wrong! When I was a half-mile away, Ricky saw me from the top and ran down to me.

"Konan!" he yelled.

"Rugggy," I yelled out, unable to pronounce "Ricky."

"You look terrible! I can't wait to hear the story," he said optimistically.

Ricky and I walked the last half mile of the challenge together, my feet finally made it to the flat ground above the canyon, and I officially conquered the Rim to Rim to Rim Challenge. We sat in the car with my head pounding. Ricky started driving and asked me what I wanted to do. There was nothing that I wanted more in the world than a McDonald's Frappe. As we drove, I sipped on some Gatorade and in no time opened the door to throw it up again. I knew that I was dehydrated but was also so hungry that I wanted to smash some food anyways. I drank that Frappe and it was heavenly. I also ate some fast food, which I was able to hold down, thankfully.

We stayed in a hotel room that night while my body recovered. I drank as much water as my body had the capacity to handle. In fact,

I woke up in the middle of the night on purpose just to chug more water. But here's what was crazy: I didn't have to use the facilities until 3 p.m. the next afternoon. My body had lost so much fluid that it took that long just to replenish it.

You can damage yourself pretty badly during an adventure like this. I was thankful that my body bounced back. I was also thankful that I gutted out the Rim to Rim to Rim Challenge and conquered it. It required more out of me than I could have ever imagined, but it also taught me more about myself than I could have ever imagined.

ADVENTURE GUIDE TIP

The last seven miles up the canyon was probably the hardest stretch of any adventure I've ever faced. I was definitely in danger of severe dehydration and even death if my physical state took a turn for the worse. I'm not sure if I even realized it at the moment, but there was something driving me to finish that challenge. For some reason, stopping short felt unacceptable. There was a need deep inside of my soul to prove myself to myself. I desperately needed to know my capabilities. It was more than just an adventure; I desired answers to the deep questions of my life. The only way that those answers could surface was through the context of a grueling challenge. The Adventure Guide Tip for this chapter is one that will help you do some soul-searching:

YOU DON'T ANSWER DEEP QUESTIONS IN SHALLOW PLACES.

Like I said, the Grand Canyon was a proving ground for myself. I had grown up with a healthy family led by incredible parents. There was nothing inside of me that felt the need to earn their attention or affirmation. But for whatever reason, I felt like I needed to answer the question: "What do you really have inside of yourself?"

A question like that is difficult to answer because you don't really know what's inside of you until you're squeezed enough for it to come out. **Pressure has an amazing ability to reveal what is concealed.** Most people never answer the deep questions they have about their identity or matters of the heart because they aren't willing to walk through the pressure. The lack of squeezing produces a lack of clarity.

Staying in shallow places equates to living surface-level. Life-altering development is found in the deep places. From my experience, I've found there are a few questions that deep places help provide answers for:

1. What are my limitations?

I've always been fascinated by my limitations. There are so many stories and movies about people who are tortured for their beliefs or some important piece of information that they have. Some of the people in those stories have a shallow breaking point, while others don't seem to even have one at all.

During self-reflection, I've always contemplated my breaking point—where my physical and mental limits actually were. For me, my breaking point went a long way in answering the question of what I really had inside. That's one of the reasons I pushed myself so hard to make it up that canyon wall. I desperately want to be a person who gives my all to follow through on the things I've set out to do.

A great question to ask yourself during self-reflection is: *What are my limits?* It reveals what we truly stand for and what we are actually committed to. Whatever you love the most, you'll endure the most for. How much are you willing to endure to fight for your faith, family, or friends? Are you willing to go to battle to see your dreams come true and make the world a better place? Our limitations are one of the greatest teachers of what we're actually about as people.

2. What are my motivations?

I've always considered myself a driven person. That's one of the reasons I've participated in so many adventures. The question that I had to face during the Rim to Rim to Rim Challenge was: *Where does my drive come from?*

We live in a culture that celebrates drive. Trust me, sometimes that's rightfully so. Without drive, we wouldn't get much accomplished and our lives wouldn't leave much of a legacy. It's a useful tool. But there's also a type of drive that can be destructive. What's the difference? The source of where your drive comes from. In other words, our motivation.

Here's a great question to answer when trying to decide whether your motivation is healthy or unhealthy: **Am I running *to* something or am I running *from* something?**

Sometimes we *run to* people's approval or fulfillment from achievement. It's easy to fall into a trap of thinking: *If I get more likes on social media, I'll finally be content.* Or maybe some of you have thought: *If I can just get that job promotion, then I'll finally feel important.* Running to something reveals the unhealthiness of our motivation.

In the same way, we often *run from* some of our deepest pain and fear. Sometimes we don't even realize that we're doing it. People pursue colleges that they're overqualified for because they think they might fail at a more challenging school. Others were hurt by their parents as children and treat themselves poorly as adults because they think they aren't worth much. Running from the challenges of life also proves that we're motivated in an unhealthy way.

How do we know if our motivation is healthy? When we're living a life of love: loving ourselves, loving others, and loving what we do. When the motivation of our drive is love within the context of our families, teams, schools, passions, and jobs, we accomplish from a place that's healthy and whole. We are no longer running *for* love, but *from* a place of love. When we can do that, we don't destroy ourselves, or those around us, trying to get where we want to go.

There's a deeper motivation behind everything that we do. If I could encourage you in any way, it would be to examine the source of that motivation. The healthiest version of you will live out the best version of your adventure. However, to become healthy, it requires that you face some pain, fear, and issues of the heart. It's hard visiting the deep places. It was hard running through the depths of the Grand Canyon. But in the same way that I came out with answers, you will, too!

ADVENTURE APPLICATION

1. What deep questions do you have about yourself that are currently unanswered?

2. What is your breaking point? Does it reveal anything about the person who you really are inside?

3. Are you currently running to something or from something? What pain or fear might be motivating you that you need to face and heal from?

ADVENTURE #4

CLIMBING KILIMANJARO

CHAPTER 12

DEVELOPING VISION

The itch to climb Mount Kilimanjaro began while I was finalizing the details to do missionary work in Tanzania, Africa. I received my flight itinerary a month before the trip and, to my surprise, our group was flying into Kilimanjaro Airport. I wondered to myself: *Kilimanjaro—the same place where Mount Kilimanjaro is?* I had never put it together that Kilimanjaro was in Tanzania until then. Sure enough, Google confirmed that I'd be just hours away from the highest mountain in Africa.

Just to get a plane ticket to Africa was a couple grand, and it's not like I traveled there frequently. I realized that this might be my one opportunity to climb Kilimanjaro, which was a bucket list item for me. There was a four day period at the end of our group's two-week trip that was set aside for tourism. We were scheduled to go see the Serengeti Plain and hang out in the bush—a vast, but also beautiful expanse of desert plains. I saw a small window of time that I might be able to sneak away from the group for a few days and conquer Kilimanjaro.

The peak of the mountain stands 19,341 feet tall.[1] People travel from all over the world to attempt to reach the summit; it has actually become one of Tanzania's major economical engines. Everyone who attempts the climb pays for a guide and a sherpa. Guides are experienced climbers who lead individuals or groups of people to the peak. Sherpas carry the gear, prepare meals, and make sure everyone stays hydrated.

Those attempting to climb the mountain choose a route that's been pre-mapped out according to time frame. The more days a climb takes, the easier the journey; the fewer days, the more difficult the climb. The biggest reason is not just the mileage but the need to acclimate to the altitude. A good climber can finish in five days, while a less experienced climber usually takes about seven to nine days. I was going to attempt to climb to the peak and back down in three days. I knew that three days would stretch me to my limits, but I also had a plane back home to catch! It was three days or bust.

I started emailing some of the companies who hosted the climbing tours in Tanzania before the trip, and none of them would take on the challenge of a three-day climb with me. Most of them asked me if I was a professional climber. I wasn't, but tried to reason with them by sharing some of the other adventures I'd conquered. They were completely uninterested. It seemed as if I was too big of a liability for them to take on. Finally, I had a breakthrough conversation with one of the climbing tour companies:

"Sir, are you willing to sign a waiver?" the person on the other side of the telephone asked me.

"Absolutely," I responded hopefully. "I'll take it a step further. If at any point, the guide says that I'm incapacitated, he can pull me off the mountain and I'll comply. I just want a shot at this."

They checked one more time, just to make sure: "Okay, just so you know. You could die. And it won't be our fault. Are you positive that you want to try this?"

"Send the waiver!" I said enthusiastically. Obviously, I had become a little too accustomed to risking my life through all of my previous adventures!

After a week-and-a-half of mission work, a bus took me to the base of Mount Kilimanjaro. My guide, who's name was Godfrey, rode with me so that we could plan our route. Supposedly he was one of the strongest and most experienced climbers that Kilimanjaro had to offer. He spoke broken English, but it was good enough for us to communicate.

"Five days," he said while holding up the five fingers on his hand.

"No, Godfrey, three days," I corrected him while waving three fingers at him to make sure that he understood.

"Three days? Nobody does it in three days," he replied sternly, also looking at me as if I was a little crazy.

"Godfrey, I don't have five days," I said back in the most convincing way that I could. "My plane leaves in three days, which means that we need to finish this climb in three days!"

My persuasive reasoning was met with a skeptical look from Godfrey. I'm not sure if he couldn't understand me, if he thought I was crazy, or maybe a combination of both. I decided to try to convince him in a different way.

"Godfrey," I looked him dead in the eyes. "Your boss told me that you are the strongest climber in all of Tanzania. We will climb this mountain in three days."

"Oh yeah, I'm very strong," Godfrey replied back enthusiastically. "I'll call my boss."

Godfrey called his boss and came back with some of the best news that I've ever heard in my life: "Okay, three days. But when we go through the check stations, do not say anything. I will do all the talking."

It dawned on me that this might even be an illegal climb. But I didn't care. I was about to attempt something that not many people had attempted before. Should I have listened to the warnings of Godfrey and the other locals? I was about to find out.

I waited at the base of the mountain as Godfrey and my sherpa, Masimba, prepared to take off. Masimba was a *tough* 60-year-old dude. I actually brought more gear than I normally would have because I knew somebody else would be carrying some of it up the mountain. Masimba often climbed ahead of us, taking a different route, making sure that food and meals were waiting for us along the way. He was a quiet guy, but I'm thankful for how hard he worked during the trip.

I waited at the base of the mountain for these guys to get ready for what felt like a very long time. They don't have the same timetable in Tanzania that I was used to in America. Their pace was the definition of lax. *Dude, my plane leaves in three days*, I thought to myself while trying not to grow impatient. Finally, everyone was ready and we took off on our climb.

During the climb, you pass through three different climate zones due to elevation. The base of the mountain is like a rainforest while the peak of it is like a frozen tundra. The vegetation at the beginning of the climb is dense, but at the top, nothing is able to grow at all. It's a pretty intense change to experience in just a few hours.

The beginning of the climb wasn't overly exhausting. Honestly, I felt like I was just walking along a trail through the forest. The constant uphill was tough on my calves, but nothing that I hadn't experienced before.

The competitor inside of me wanted to move faster. I'd attempt to increase our pace, but everytime Godfrey would call out to me: "Pole, pole!" That's the way to say "slow" in Swahili. He also called me *rafiki* continuously. I thought that he was calling me the monkey from Lion King, but I found out that *rafiki* actually means friend.

Godfrey was being a good guide by getting me to slow down. He was an experienced climber, and therefore knew what to expect during later stages of the climb. I had no clue what we were about to face, but he knew exactly what we were in for. He paced me, and in retrospect, I'm very thankful.

The route that we chose had several checkpoints along the way. These were places where climbers would typically eat, relax, and get some sleep for the night. We obviously couldn't afford to stop at all of the checkpoints or we would never hit our goal of three days. When we approached the first checkpoint, the worker asked Godfrey a question in Swahili and I heard Godfrey say: "Five days." The worker shook his head and then we were again on our way.

Before much longer, we hit the second checkpoint. I was ready to press on to the next one, as we still had some daylight ahead of us. But Godfrey said we were staying for the night, and he was the man in charge. I slept inside of a *Shakti*-looking, A-frame hut that wasn't much larger than a small bedroom. If you aren't comfortable sleeping right next to strangers, then climbing Kilimanjaro probably isn't the adventure for you. I spent the night laying right next to four dudes who were complete and total strangers.

Godfrey knocked on my door early the next morning as the

sun was coming up. Masimba cooked us a delicious breakfast; our bodies would end up needing that fuel as the day went on. We blew past another checkpoint. By now, the word about us attempting to conquer the mountain in three days had spread among the other guides and groups of climbers. Whenever we passed them, they would silently pump their fists in the air and give us high fives. They encouraged us while trying to keep the whole thing hush-hush so we didn't get busted.

Although the climb would soon become physically taxing, up to this point, the biggest challenge for me was blindly following Godfrey, unsure of what was coming next. A lot of the hike is through the rainforest. Because of the dense vegetation, you're making progress but can't really see that you're making progress. Every once in a while, I'd see a peak through a sliver of open space between trees.

"Godfrey, is that it?!" I'd ask excitedly.

"Not yet," he'd respond in a manner that was cool, calm, and collected.

I knew that we were headed in the right direction, but because the end wasn't in sight, the entire adventure began to feel like a struggle. Finally, the peak of Kilimanjaro came into view. All of a sudden, I felt recharged and refocused. A challenging journey was still ahead of us. But I could see where we were going. And I now knew that we could get there.

ADVENTURE GUIDE TIP

I learned a valuable lesson while climbing up Kilimanjaro. Whenever the peak was hidden from sight, the hike felt like more of a struggle. But whenever the peak came into sight, it felt like I was at my strongest. Physically, nothing about the difficulty of the climb had changed. What was the only difference? Vision. The ability to see where we were headed—our ultimate goal.

Many of you may never climb Kilimanjaro. However, we all

have goals, or places in life, that we are trying to reach. Any goal that's actually worth striving for includes a climb. During that climb, there's something about vision that makes a huge difference. When our goals get out of focus, we struggle. But when the finish line is within our line of sight, we adventure forward with strength and courage. Here's our Adventure Guide Tip for this chapter:

WHAT WE SEE DETERMINES HOW WE STEP.

Here's my definition of vision: *a picture of your preferred future*. In other words, if you were to imagine exactly what you'd want your future to look like when it comes to family, career, passion, and adventure, what would that picture look like? If you can see it, that means you have vision.

Those who have vision in life are people who know exactly where they want to go. In other words, they can *see* it. And because they can see it, they know exactly where and how to step. They have a defined target to aim their energy and effort toward.

If you've ever been around a great visionary, you probably know them to be people who are motivated, hopeful, and purposeful. Their movement always seems to be inspired and intentional. On the other hand, people that lack vision seem to aimlessly wander through life. They aren't sure where they are headed. And because they don't know where they are going, they obviously have no clue how to get there. **Vision is the difference between a life of survival**

and a life of significance.

I want to address those of you who feel like your vision is a little bit cloudy right now. Don't worry, you can still live the life you've always wanted. It takes time to figure out what we're truly passionate about. It's a life-long journey and our values become clearer the further we walk along that journey. But here are some tips to help you as you're working to see vision more clearly:

1. Open doors and look around.

We're all presented with doors of opportunity through the course of our lives. Oftentimes, they require commitment from us that we aren't sure if we want to make yet. Here's the rule of thumb that I live by: it doesn't hurt to at least open the door and look around.

How can we know that we are passionate about something if we never try it out? **It's through learning what we don't like that we discover what we love.** The first job offer that you get out of college might not be your dream job, but it doesn't hurt to interview. Perhaps it's exercise. You might discover that you're more of a biker than a runner, but it won't kill you to start exercising and figure it out as you go along.

Every door is an opportunity and every opportunity is an experiment. Experiments are exceptional tools to help us develop vision.

2. Serve people.

It's selflessness, not selfishness, that creates contentment. The point of our lives is not to make our own lives better, but make the lives of those around us better. Ironically, when we make the lives of others better, it inevitably makes our own lives better as well.

Here's a great question to ask yourself: *How can I make the biggest difference for others?* In his book, *Good to Great,* Jim Collins encourages us to focus on the areas where our gifts, passions, and ability to make money collide.[2]

I like that formula, but I'd tweak it slightly for myself. I believe that God placed every single one of us on the planet because he has placed a *calling* on our lives. In other words, he has planned and prepared specific ways that we can change the lives of those around us. Think of it like this: your *calling* is like a road. It shows you the direction you are supposed to go. The *gifts* that you have are like a vehicle—they help you travel down the road. And last but not least, your *passion* is like gasoline that helps to keep you moving forward.

When vision revolves around yourself, it's extremely difficult to make decisions about the direction you want to go. Maybe you want to be successful, make money, or chase popularity. But when your vision revolves around other people, it becomes much easier to clarify how you can impact the world.

Once the vision for your life starts to become clear—and I promise that it will—the best thing you can do is work backwards. When it comes to vision, we must see the big goal but start with small steps. For example, when I decided that I wanted to climb Kilimanjaro, there were a lot of steps that needed to be taken before reaching the summit. I had to follow Godfrey. But before I could follow Godfrey, I had to hire him. Before I could hire him, I had to talk to his boss. Before I could talk to his boss, I had to make a call. Before I made the call, I had to buy a plane ticket.

When you work backward and break your vision into small steps, what seems impossible becomes attainable. In the same way that I climbed Kilimanjaro, you can climb toward the picture of your preferred future. It's as simple as seeing and stepping.

ADVENTURE APPLICATION

1. What do you think your calling, gifts, and passions are?

2. What have you tried out that you don't enjoy? Does that say anything about what you might actually enjoy?

3. If you have a vision for your life, try working backward and writing out the steps that will help you get there. Try breaking them down in a way that's realistic and attainable.

CHAPTER 13

ENJOYING THE JOURNEY

Godfrey's goal was to reach the highest checkpoint of Kilimanjaro during the afternoon of day number two. Once there, we would eat, catch some sleep, and then start our ascent to the peak in the middle of the night. This was the most common summiting strategy deployed by climbers. When you leave the checkpoint at midnight you can usually make it to the peak right at sunrise.

I think that Godfrey saw I wasn't the typical climber. In fact, he called me *wazimu*, which means *crazy*, many times throughout our adventure. When we reached the highest checkpoint early in the afternoon, I convinced him to change our strategy.

"You are very fast," he said to me, looking semi-impressed.

"I can go faster than this Godfrey!" I responded enthusiastically.

So we ate a quick lunch, packed our cold weather gear, and marched on toward the summit. There would be nobody else on the route to the peak besides me and Godfrey. We were headed into the most challenging part of the climb completely alone. And I had no clue just how dangerous and gut-wrenching it would actually be.

Mount Kilimanjaro is actually an inactive volcano. The sides of the mountain are cinder, which makes for very loose footing. Every time you move a couple of feet forward, you slide a foot backwards. Every step was difficult. It makes the journey not only physically grueling but also mentally grueling. You feel like you're trying to progress with everything inside of you but, no matter what you do, you keep getting pushed back. It doesn't matter how quickly you get to the last leg of the climb, it's a slow journey to the top from there.

But we climbed ahead. From 15,000 feet; to 16,000 feet; to 17,000 feet; to 18,000 feet. And at about 18,500 feet, the wheels fell off for me.

The altitude, combined with little rest coming up the mountain, hit me like a ton of bricks. All of a sudden, it felt like my head was in a vice and it was challenging to breathe. I found myself shuffling like an old man. This is why most climbers take a minimum of five days to climb Kilimanjaro. It's not necessarily the difficulty of the climb that gets you, it's your body not adjusting quickly enough to the altitude. I shuffled a little farther and paused to throw up as I battled through a terrible migraine. I know, I know—no surprise there! Puking seems to be the one thing I can count on happening throughout all of my adventures.

Like I said earlier, you climb your way through three major climate changes on Kilimanjaro. The last one is by far the worst. The base of the mountain was sunny and warm; the peak had winter-like weather. We crested over the top of the rim and stopped to put on pants, jackets, and hats as the temperature fell to 20° Fahrenheit when the wind began to blow. On top of that, when we were about a half-mile from the peak, a storm rolled over the mountaintop. It started snowing hard and the wind was blowing furiously. We were now hiking in whiteout conditions.

Honestly, something snapped inside of me and I started to get pretty freaked out. Storms can be extremely dangerous on mountaintops. Plus, Godfrey and I were up there all alone. I was extremely weak from the altitude sickness; as I shivered uncontrollably, I looked over at Godfrey, and could tell that he was gassed as well. The reality that nobody was coming to help us hit me with excruciating intensity. I was getting colder by the moment and was beginning to fear hypothermia setting in. The snow was so thick that Godfrey and I could now barely see each other. In a moment of panic, I took off running. It's said that whenever people face fear, they'll respond in one of two ways: fight or flight. I chose flight.

It was like a scene from a horror movie. You would have thought that an invisible killer was chasing me with a knife. I was running and could barely hear Godfrey trying to say something over the wind. I was so distraught, tears began streaming down my face!

I ran to what I thought was the peak and started to celebrate, just to find out that it wasn't the real peak at all. The wind continued to hammer as I took off running once again in whiteout conditions. Fear was beginning to grip me. In a moment of desperation, I cried out to God to remove the storm. Honestly, I was not sure how much more of the frigid wind and snow I could handle. Finally, I could see the sign at the peak through the blizzard-Iike conditions. Almost miraculously, like out of a movie, the wind stopped and the sun came out! It was an emotional moment. Tears were running down my face, as I was so grateful to be standing on the peak.

I soaked in the experience of being at the tippy-top of Mount Kilimanjaro. I knew that I'd probably never be back again. At 19,341 feet, you can see unobstructed for what seems like forever. I pulled out my iPhone to capture the view with a picture, and of course, my phone was too cold to actually be used. Thank goodness I had brought a mini camera as well. I was able to snap some pictures to remember the moment.

Absorbing the mountain top experience was surreal but also short-lived. Something that most people don't realize is how little oxygen is available at that elevation. The air is extremely thin, and it's hard to breathe when you're just standing there. Even when you take deep breaths, it seems like it's never enough. I also remembered that we had several more hours of descent to make it to the highest camp for the night at 14,000 feet.

My altitude sickness stuck with me as we began our climb back down the mountain. I had burned through all of my water on the way up. It wasn't even because I was thirsty, but it was so cold that I was forced to drink every thirty seconds to prevent the tube of my CamelBak from freezing. Godfrey was my savior on the trip! Thank God, he had some extra water and was kind enough to let me take two huge, heavenly gulps. I also started losing motor skills on the way down. In fact, on several occasions I tripped and slid down the steep embankment on my butt. It wasn't a pretty sight and I knew I was in pretty rough shape. You know it's bad when your guide is wobbly too.

We arrived at the highest camp near 10 p.m. At the time of our arrival, another group was about to begin their summit bid. Godfrey and I received a lot of high fives and atta-boys from the other climbers and guides. I slept that night with a migraine as my body was slowly decompressing from the altitude. It felt so amazing to be able to curl up in my warm sleeping bag to end the second day.

In the morning, the migraine lingered with me, but overall, I was feeling better. Before we took off that morning, Godfrey pulled me aside and tried to convince me to cut our journey short.

"Here's what we're going to do," he said convincingly. "They have made a new route. They can bring a truck and pick you up here. You have already summited, friend."

"Godfrey, it'll be a cold day in heck before I let that happen!" I smiled and said. "We have to finish what we started!"

Godfrey had no words. He just shook his head. The truth was that Godfrey was struggling as well, but as the guide, he didn't want to show it. If the strongest guide is having a hard time, you know that you're in trouble. It wasn't until we reached the bottom that Godfrey admitted to me that he was "getting a little wobbly on the mountain."

We finished the climb, from start to finish, in two-half days plus one full day.. My headache continued to linger through the flight home the next day. But I had done it. I conquered Kilimanjaro.

ADVENTURE GUIDE TIP

I was so motivated to reach the top of Kilimanjaro. And don't get me wrong, looking out from the top of the mountain was an incredible experience. But whenever I think back on the adventure, most of my memories come from the climb, the descent, and my time with Godfrey. Ninety-nine-percent of the experience revolved around the journey, not the destination. That leads us to our Adventure Guide Tip for this chapter:

THE JOURNEY IS THE DESTINATION.

We live in a culture that celebrates success. The destination, summit, and pinnacle are what people pay attention to and praise the most. And that's not necessarily a bad thing. However, even among the most successful people in the world, 99-percent of life is spent climbing through the journey. Very little time is spent on podiums and accumulating accolades.

Why does all of this matter? It's easy to become so obsessed with the destination that we forget to enjoy the journey. And if you don't enjoy the journey, unfortunately, your life is going to be pretty miserable. Ninety-nine-percent of life is the journey, after all. If moments of success are the only ones that make you content, you're going to be discontent 99-percent of the time!

We often misunderstand the smile on a quarterback's face after they've led their team to a championship, or a businessman's face after finally becoming profitable. We think: *Wow, their life must be great all of the time.* After conquering some pretty big challenges in my own life, I've learned to think about it differently. It's important to remember that there's a journey behind every trophy. When you look at a winner, you're seeing the joy of victory, but aren't always aware of the difficulties of their climb to the summit.

If you were to see the selfies that I snapped while on top of Kilimanjaro, you'd likely assume that it was a mountaintop moment. In some ways it was—after all, I was literally on a mountaintop! But behind my smile was an excruciating migraine and fear about making it back down. It took everything inside of me to stop shivering for ten seconds to even take the picture. I reached the top, but it was a heck of a journey to get there.

Let me encourage you: **don't compare your journey to somebody's mountaintop.** They've faced challenges, struggle, and pain just like you have. But people don't usually share that part of their stories. They focus on the good, which leads us to believe the lie that it's always been good. It leads us to believe that our struggle means we are doing something wrong—which simply isn't true!

Reaching a goal can be gratifying, but it doesn't complete you or fix the problems of your life. Moments of success are fun, but they're exactly that—just moments. They don't last forever. Every year, a new champion is crowned. New movies are always rising to the top of box office sales. New songs are constantly reaching the top of the charts. New businesses quickly become the most innovative. Being at the top is only temporary. It's impossible to stay there!

Society has believed the lie that success will make everything better. Working hard to pursue success is admirable, but you will still be you afterwards. I went from summiting Kilimanjaro to tripping and sliding down the mountain on my butt multiple times. But for me, it was all a part of the journey. Every journey has ups and downs. We become discouraged about the downs, but they are what make the best memories.

Ninety-nine-percent of every adventure is about the journey. Let's learn to enjoy it!

ADVENTURE APPLICATION

1. Do you have a hard time enjoying the journey? If your answer is yes, why do you think that is?

2. Who do you view as successful? Think about all of the steps that went into their journey of becoming successful. If you struggle with contentment, try to remember their journey the next time you feel like things are moving too slowly.

ADVENTURE #5

THE GREATEST ADVENTURE

CHAPTER 14

THE END OF YOUR ROPE

I want to congratulate those of you who have stuck with me and read this far. It says a lot about who you are. You have the type of hunger, discipline, and grit needed to live your adventure to the fullest. Before we part ways, I want to share about my greatest adventure. It's been more exciting and life-changing than all of my other adventures combined. I hope by the end of this chapter, you'll decide to join me on this adventure as well.

It's time for me to come clean. I've had an unfair advantage during every adventure that I've told you about through this book: the ultramarathon, the Tour Divide, the Rim to Rim to Rim Challenge, and climbing Kilimanjaro. I've actually had an unfair advantage in every adventure of life.

I grew up as a pastor's kid. For many, that might be a negative experience, but for me, it was the best-case scenario. Many pastor's kids that I've had conversations with admit that they'd see one version of their parents at church, but at home, they acted like entirely different people. In other words, they never practiced what they preached. That wasn't the case with my parents. They didn't just teach me about God, they lived out their relationship with Him. They were the exact same people whether they were on the platform or just hanging out at home. Dad and Mom were the first people to really model just how much God loved me by the way they treated me.

My parents and I had so many conversations about following Jesus when I was a kid. They'd always tell me: "Son, if you're going to have a relationship with God, it has to be your own, not ours. Whenever you stand before Him at the end of your life, it's just going to be you. We don't want you to follow Him just because we do, but rather, because you want to. Now, we pray that you've seen his love through us and want a relationship with Him. But at the end of the day, your faith has to be your own."

Since a young age, my faith was my own. I was the kid who told his entire kindergarten class about Jesus. In high school, my friends knew that I was a Christian. In college, I'd teach Sunday school every Sunday morning. Now I'm the pastor of a church in Columbus, Ohio.

I've always had a relationship with God and wanted the same for others. You might be wondering why that is. I've found that there's nothing more life-changing than the love of God. Many of you reading this might have different ideas of who God is based on sermons you've heard or Christians that you know. The best way that I can describe God from getting to know Him over the course of my entire life is as a loving *Father*.

One of the best verses in the Bible is John 1:12. It says, "But to all who believed Him and accepted Him, He gave the right to become children of God" (NLT). Everyone who accepts a relationship with God literally becomes His child. It's a relationship that's personal, genuine, and intimate.

With kids of my own, I have experience being a father. The love that I have for all of them is too deep for me to even attempt to explain. It's not because of what they do, but because of whose they are. They are mine and belong to me. I remember holding them for the first time and wondering to myself: *Why do I love them so much? I have to change their diapers. They steal my sleep. They cost a lot of money. And they don't bring any income into this household.* But none of that mattered. I loved them simply because they were my kids.

God looks at his kids in the exact same way. Most of us have no clue how deep His love runs for us. His heart's desire is to be active and involved in every single detail of his kids' lives—to support, lead, and fight for them. And it's not based on our ability, but instead our willingness to give Him access to our lives.

I have a tattoo on my arm that says: "Christ in me." It reminds me of the truth that God is living on the inside of me. He's not in a galaxy far, far away, distant and detached from the details of my life. He's a father who is not only close but also concerned about every single one of life's challenges.

That's why I said that I had an unfair advantage during my adventures. Take the Tour Divide for example. I wasn't alone. I had a relationship with God, and unfortunately, some of the others didn't know Him. During some of the toughest moments, people were breaking down mentally: cussing, screaming, and throwing stuff. Trust me, the challenges weren't any easier for me than they were for anybody else. But God, my Father, was with me in the lowest moments. He made all of the difference.

The toughest times of those adventures have actually taught me the most about God. Battling through the beginning stages of hypothermia, altitude sickness, and heat exhaustion were vulnerable and emotional. But ironically, they were also the moments I felt the closest to God. Weakness has a way of tearing your walls down. I knew that I needed Him, and every single time, He showed up. There were moments when tears streamed down my face because of His faithfulness, tangible love, and peace in difficult moments.

Adventures have a way of reminding you of your humanity and mortality. Even the most physically, mentally, and emotionally strong people in the world have limits. Anybody can be brought to their knees while facing hypothermia, altitude sickness, or severe injury. It doesn't matter how tough you are! Whenever you come face-to-face with your limitations during an adventure—whether physical, mental, or emotional—you hit a breaking point. Everybody has one.

I've found that the adventure of life works the same way. Regardless of how great your family, your friends, or your job are, difficulty is inevitable. I don't know what your difficulties are, but I do know that you have them. Some of you may have struggled with mental health for years. Others may have suffered the loss of family members. Maybe you've experienced a crushing divorce. Difficulty, understandably so, brings us to our breaking points.

The question is: *What happens when you reach your breaking point? Is it just over? Is life now destined to be full of discouragement and despair?*

It doesn't have to be that way! Hang with me for a little bit longer; there's reason for hope!

ADVENTURE GUIDE TIP

Whenever we come to the end of our rope, there's another rope that we have the opportunity to grab. It's a rope that God extended to us, and it leads to a relationship with Him. It's the type of relationship that provides unlimited help through every situation and circumstance in life. Why? Simply because of the unconditional love of your Heavenly Father. Here's our last and best Adventure Guide Tip yet:

WHERE MY STRENGTH STOPS, GOD'S STRENGTH STARTS.

The Bible is the book we can read to learn more about who God is and how much He loves us. And it has a lot to say about how His affection plays out. One of the author's of the Bible is a guy named Paul. He traveled the world planting churches, preaching about Jesus, and even wrote two-thirds of the New Testament. He was persecuted for his faith, and often ended up getting arrested, beaten, and imprisoned. On a few occasions, people even tried to kill him. It was an adventurous life to say the least. But God spoke many things to him through the many adventures. In the book of 2 Corinthians, Paul shared one a lesson that can really help us:

Each time he said, "My grace is all you need. My power works best in weakness..." (2 Corinthians 12:9, NLT)

Paul was actually sharing a conversation that he had with God, his Father. Although Paul is not specific about the source of his pain, he shared that there was a difficulty in his life that refused to leave him alone. It drove him to prayer. Knowing that he didn't have the strength to endure, he asked God if he could remove the struggle. God responded by letting Paul know that the power of God actually works best in our weakness.

It's a perfect reflection of the father-child relationship that God wants to have with us. We are limited but our Father is limitless. We are sometimes weak but our Father is always strong. We are broken but our Father is whole.

You might be asking: *Konan, how do I go about starting this type of relationship with God?* Well, I'm glad you asked! There are no prerequisites or qualifications. It's not a job that you have to apply for. You don't have to clean yourself up or fix all of your mistakes before you come to God. The truth is, He already did for us what we could never do for ourselves.

Since the beginning of time, humanity has proven their weakness over and over again. We've all sinned against God, ourselves, and made the same mistakes over and over again. Unfortunately, sin is the thing that separates us from God. Whenever we sin, we choose our broken way over God's perfect way. The truth is, we are sinful people who live in a sinful world. We are incapable of avoiding sin and will never be perfect.

God knows your weaknesses and flaws. He's completely aware of every mistake that you've ever made and loves you anyway. In fact, He's crazy about you! That's why He's provided a way for us, imperfect people, to have a relationship with Him, a perfect Father.

A little bit over 2,000 years ago, He sent His one and only Son, who's name was Jesus, to the world. Jesus never sinned, but took our sin upon His shoulders as His own. He paid the price that our sin required by dying as a perfect sacrifice on the cross. Three days later, He rose from the dead, defeating the sin that should have killed him and should have punished us. When He did so, He released us from our guilty sentence. We can overcome because He overcame! Now, whoever accepts a relationship with Him is no longer viewed as a sinner, but accepted as a son or daughter who has been completely forgiven. Because of Jesus, our sin no longer has to separate us from God. He lives inside of us, adventures with us, and helps us navigate all of life's challenges. It's a relationship that starts right now on earth and lasts through eternity in Heaven when you move on from this life. He loves you so much that he desires to be in a perfect relationship with you for the rest of eternity!

If you get nothing else from this book, please understand this: following Jesus is the greatest adventure of life. Because of His deep love for you, He has plans and purposes for you that are so much greater than you could ever imagine. You might never run 100 miles or climb Kilimanjaro, but I guarantee that the love of God will take you on a wild ride!

ADVENTURE APPLICATION

1. Are you far from God?

If the answer to that question is yes, let me encourage you. He doesn't want to be far from you any longer. Sometimes it can feel like you and God are both standing on cliffs, but they are 1,000 feet apart from each other. Even if you wanted to get to Him, you couldn't! The cross of Jesus is the bridge that allows you to get to God. Jesus' death on the cross proves the Father's love for you and has the ability to restore your relationship with Him.

2. Do you want to accept a relationship with Jesus?

You don't have to wait any longer. 1 John 1:9 says, "But if we confess our sins to Him, He is faithful and just to forgive us our sins and to cleanse us from all wickedness" (NLT). That means that if we believe in Jesus, confess our sin to Him, and accept Him as Lord and Savior, then we can have eternal relationship with Him because we are officially forgiven and officially children. If you're ready to start that kind of relationship with Jesus, pray this prayer:

"Jesus, I admit that I'm a sinner and ask for You to forgive me for my sin. I believe that You died on the cross, rose from the grave, and are the Savior of the universe. Today, I accept You as my Lord and Savior and can't wait to start a relationship with You!

In these final moments together, if you would give me the honor, I'd love to speak a blessing over you:

May the things that once held you back be broken over your life. May every negative word and all shame of the past melt off of you now.
May all the fear, anxiety, and people-pleasing that once held you captive, hold you captive no longer.
Today, may you understand just how much you are loved.
May it sink in that there is nothing that you can do to make Him love you any less or any more.
May you know that you were created by God with a purpose and plan.
Your future is bright, and there are new beginnings ahead of you.
From this day forward, you are fearless, courageous, and bold.
You will never be alone but will always walk in a relationship with the God of the universe.
It's a new day in your life.

May the love and peace of God saturate your soul, and may you see His divine beauty everywhere you look.

May His favor and blessing rest upon your life, in Jesus' name!

Now...GO LIVE YOUR ADVENTURE!

FAVORITE QUOTES FROM ADVENTUROUS FRIENDS

Patrick Robinson
"The unexamined life is not worth living."[1]

Lindsay Butterfield
"Expectations are an invitation for resentment."

E. Scott Harvey
"Create your life, don't just accept it."

Jen Roenker
"I choose to live to inspire and not impress."

BrieAnna Reedus
"Comfort is the enemy of progress."[2]

Mike Samuelson
"Fear is an incompetent teacher."[3]

Tim Weddington
"The mountains of today are the molehills of tomorrow."[4]

Crystal Lowe
"Just because you can doesn't mean you should."

Karen Vreeland
"Worry is a cycle of inefficient thoughts whirling around a center of fear."[5]

Clint Curry
"A wise man is quick to listen and slow to speak and slow to get angry." (James 1:19)

Chris Martin
"Don't talk about it, be about it."[6]
"Do what is right, not what is easy."[7]

Barb Bates
"The pessimist sees the difficulty in every opportunity; the optimist sees the opportunity in every difficulty."[8]

Heather O'Leary
"Worry is like a rocking chair. It keeps moving but doesn't get you anywhere."[9]

Kendra Hinkle
"Face it, forgive it, move forward, and then you will forget it."

Kaden Stephens
"If you enjoy the challenge of the day, you can have a lot of fun."

My Coach, Jerry Fresanko
"Control the controllables."

Jennifer Stephens
"Live to give."

NOTES

Chapter 2

1. Geoff Loftus, "If You're Going Through Hell, Keep Going - Winston Churchill," *Forbes*. May 9, 2012. https://www.forbes.com/sites/geoffloftus/2012/05/09/if-youre-going-throug h-hell-keep-going-winston-churchill/?sh=6dd09a59d549_
2. Martin Luther King, Jr. "'Keep Moving from This Mountain' - Address at Spelman College on 10 April 1960," *The Martin Luther King, Jr. Research and Education Institute, Stanford University*. May 7, 2021. https://kinginstitute.stanford.edu/king-papers/documents/keep- moving-mountain-address-spelman-college-10-april-1960

Chapter 6

1. Mike Berardino, "Mike Tyson explains one of his most famous quotes," *South Florida Sun Sentinel*. November 9, 2012. https://www.sun-sentinel.com/sports/fl-xpm-2012-11-0 9-sfl-mike-tyson-explains-one-of-his-most-famous-quotes-20121109-story.html
2. Stewart Borie, "H.A.L.T. - A basic rule of decision making for success," *Inquiry International*. 2011. https://www.inquiryinternational.com/blog/halt-a-basic-rule-of-decisio n-making-for-success

Chapter 7

1. "The Route," Tour Divide. May 22, 2021. https://tourdivide.org/about_the_route

Chapter 8

1. *The Lord of the Rings Trilogy.* Directed by Peter Jackson, New Line Cinema, 2001-2003.

Chapter 9

1. "13 Things You Didn't Know About Grand Canyon National Park," *U.S. Department of the Interior.* February 23, 2017. https://www.doi.gov/blog/13-things-you-didnt-know-about-gr and-canyon-national-park
2. "Grand Canyon Rim-To-Rim Hike," *National Park Foundation.* May 22, 2021. https://ww w.nationalparks.org/connect/blog/ grand-canyon-rim-rim-hike

Chapter 12

1. "Climbing Mount Kilimanjaro," *TourRadar.* May 28, 2021. https://www.tourradar.com/hg/k ilimanjaro
2. Jim Collins, *Good to Great: Why Some Companies Make the Leap…and Others Don't* (New York, NY: HarperCollins, 2001).

Favorite Quotes

1. Plato, "Apology," *The Internet Classics Archive.* Translated by Benjamin Jowett. June 18, 2021. http://classics.mit.edu/Plato/ apology.html
2. *The Greatest Showman.* Directed by Michael Gracey, Twentieth Century Fox, 2017.

3. "Star Trek: Picard." Created by Kirsten Beyer, Michael Chabon, Akiva Goldsman, CBS Television Studios, 2020.

4. Ellis Peters, *Fallen Into the Pit* (New York, NY: Mysterious Press, 1996).

5. Marlys Popma, "They Just Don't Mix," *The Christian Conservative*. December 24, 2017. http://www.thechristianconservative.com/?p=4988

6. D.L. Lunsford, "Leaking Grace?," *D.L. Lunsford's Flight of the Butterfly*. June 15, 2021. https://dllunsfordwriter.com/2021/06/15/leaking-grace/

7. Roy T. Bennett, *The Light in the Heart: Inspirational Thoughts for Living Your Best Life* (Roy Bennett, self-published, 2016).

8. *The Fifty-First Annual Co-operative Congress*, edited by A. Whitehead. June 9-11, 1919. *Hathi Trust Digital Library*. Accessed June 19, 2021. https://babel.hathitrust.org/cgi/pt?id=uc1.b3034826&view=1up&seq=1&q1=pessimist

9. Linda Dillow, *Calm My Anxious Heart* (Colorado Springs, CO: NavPress, 1998).

AUTHOR BIO

Konan Stephens is a part-time adventurer, the full-time pastor of C3 Church, and the leader of Venture Multiplication Network, which plants churches across the country. He is a popular speaker who enjoys inspiring others to live their own adventure. When he is not working, you will find him on a run, ride, hike, or out in a tree stand. Konan loves nothing more than sharing his adventures with his wife and kids.

More resources to help you live your adventure:
goliveyouradventure.com

Follow Konan's adventure on social media:
Youtube: Konan Stephens
Instagram: @goliveyouradventure / @konanstephens
Facebook: Konan Stephens